Additional praise for *Next Move, Best Move*

"Kimberly is the voice of our generation and a trusted resource who remains true to her vision. Kimberly's commitment to career growth strategies creates an empowering space for us all to take our seat at the table."

—Pauleanna Reid, *Journalist*

"Kimberly Cummings beckons the leader in each of us to reach for our career goals and dreams, and offers insightful tools and tips to get its readers that much closer to accomplishing them. This book is also a wonderful and much-needed reminder, especially for women, that there is greatness inside of us; all we have to do is lean into it. Her career lessons are invaluable for anyone seeking to carve out their special place in the workplace."

—Samantha Hunter, Writer for Martha Stewart and *Forbes*

"Kimberly B. Cumming's *Next Move Best Move* reminds you that it is never too late to craft the career of your dreams. Reading the book is like having a relatable, candid, and supportive career and leadership coach in your ear. Through this book, Kimberly not only inspires you to action with her own narrative but most importantly delivers a clear outline, measurable steps, and specific tools that you can use to ensure 'your next move is your best move.'"

—Daniella Kahane, Executive Director/CEO, WIN SUMMIT

Next Move, Best Move

Transitioning Into a Career You'll Love

Next Move, Best Move

*Transitioning Into a Career
You'll Love*

Kimberly B. Cummings

WILEY

For general information on our other products and services or for technical support, please contact our Customer Care Department within the United States at (800) 762-2974, outside the United States at (317) 572-3993, or fax (317) 572-4002.

Wiley publishes in a variety of print and electronic formats and by print-on-demand. Some material included with standard print versions of this book may not be included in e-books or in print-on-demand. If this book refers to media such as a CD or DVD that is not included in the version you purchased, you may download this material at http://booksupport.wiley.com. For more information about Wiley products, visit www.wiley.com.

Library of Congress Cataloging-in-Publication Data is Available:

ISBN   9781119736226 (Paperback)
ISBN   9781119736240 (ePDF)
ISBN   9781119736233 (epub)

COVER DESIGN: KIMBERLY B. CUMMINGS
AUTHOR PHOTO: JEROME SHAW

SKY10025959_042721

This book is dedicated to any professional who has felt over-looked, unappreciated, and undervalued. With your next move, you have the power to change the trajectory of your career.

Contents

Foreword   xi

Definition of *Career Transition*   xiii

    Introduction   1

            Part One   11

Chapter 1: Serving as a People Leader Is a
                Privilege, Not a Rite of Passage   13

Chapter 2: Taking Stock of Your Experiences   25

            Part Two   41

Chapter 3: Core Values Are the Essence of What Make
                You Happy   43

Chapter 4: Setting Long-Term and Short-Term
                Career Goals   57

Chapter 5: Addressing Where You Are, So You Are Ready
for Where You Want to Go   73
Chapter 6: Relationships Are Still Everything   85

Part Three   **101**

Chapter 7: Building Your Career Strategy   103
Chapter 8: Your Personal and Professional "Experience" –
A Deeper Look into Personal and Professional
Branding   117

Part Four   **129**

Chapter 9: How to Bring It All Together and Put It Out
in the World   131
Chapter 10: Embracing Your Voice in the Workplace   143
Chapter 11: The Truth about Salary Negotiation   155
Chapter 12: How to Know When It's Time to Go   173
Chapter 13: Put It All Together   185

Acknowledgments   197
Index   199

Foreword

If we've learned anything from COVID-19, it's that nothing is certain. The world – including businesses, finances, and careers – can change on a dime. I don't know about you, but there were plenty of moments during the pandemic when I wished I had a personal advisor telling me how to handle it all.

Even in nonpandemic times, that would be pretty amazing, don't you think?

Well, I have good news. Kimberly B. Cummings is that advisor, and reading this book is like having Kimberly as your own personal career and leadership coach. On every page, you'll benefit from her extensive experience in university career services, corporate talent development, and diversity and inclusion. Whether you are a student, recent graduate, early or mid-career professional, Kimberly will provide you with tactical, tangible tools to achieve success and become the leader you want to be.

I first met Kimberly at a career services event where I was speaking about my second book, *Becoming the Boss*. She came up to chat after my presentation (she will teach you how to network like that!) and we began a conversation that has lasted for more than a decade over breakfasts, lunches, coffee dates, phone calls, and Zoom chats.

As you'll soon discover, one of my favorite things about Kimberly is her positivity. You'll experience this through all the personal stories she shares of her own successes and challenges and the wonderful career affirmations that start each chapter. She deeply believes that everyone – and women and people of color in particular – can create both financial success and the lifestyle they want. (And if you're not sure yet what lifestyle you want, she'll help you figure that out, too.)

Kimberly also believes that every individual can be a leader, regardless of his or her career level or specific job function. I couldn't agree more. As she writes, "Being a leader has less to do with a title and more to do with the influence you bring to the workplace." That influence is what allows you to live and work according to your values. It enables you to advocate for yourself. And it helps you to construct a reputation, relationships, and a track record of success that will extend beyond your current job.

Kimberly's business is called Manifest Yourself, and that's exactly what you'll experience on the following pages. With Kimberly's coaching, you'll begin to create a career with true longevity. No matter what happens in the world, in your industry, in your organization, and in your personal life, you'll attract opportunities and continue moving forward to achieve your goals and live the life you want.

I can't wait to see you what you accomplish.

Lindsey Pollak
New York Times bestselling author

Definition of *Career Transition*

Before we dig into the introduction of this book, I'd like to define *career transition*. Many professionals believe that a career transition means moving from one industry to another, but a transition is simply a shift from one state of your career to another. In this book's context, a *career transition* is defined as any type of career movement, such as graduating from an undergraduate or graduate-level program and shifting to your first professional job. It can also be defined as the shift of accepting a promotional or lateral opportunity at your current company, moving to a new industry, or choosing a lateral or promotional opportunity at a new company. Last but not least, a career transition can also be a mental transition from moving from being just another employee at your company to becoming a leader in your workplace.

Introduction

This book has a specific purpose.

I wrote this book for professionals who feel as though it's too late to change the trajectory of their careers. They are frustrated and contemplating how they ended up at that exact desk, in-person or virtual, when they knew they were destined for more. Many professionals have experienced that moment when they look up at the ceiling and ask, "How did I end up here?"

Even if "here" is going well, many times professionals who have been able to navigate their careers to a certain level start to look back and wonder how they can be strategic in their next career moves. For years, they may have landed job after job, but something has changed and they know it's their job to fix it.

Perhaps you feel unappreciated, overlooked, and underpaid for the talents you know you have, and you are underutilized in your current role, too. You also know that if your supervisor asks you to complete one more thing, that you're ready to give him or her a piece of your mind and tell him or her to do it instead. Better yet, your supervisor should give it to your co-worker who you know is getting paid more than you for the same work.

Or maybe you've reached a new level in your career and how you move as a professional needs to change. You're finally ready to position yourself as a leader, and you know that it's time you build your first career strategy versus relying on your manager or company to do it for you. Your next move will require something different and you're not quite sure what that is just yet.

The good news is there's a light at the end of the tunnel of this terrible thought process, and that's the fact that you recognize something isn't right. You realize you're undervalued, and you believe you are destined for more – but what is more? Luckily, this book is designed to take you to the next level in your career to achieve *more* – to a level that allows you to finally be seen as the leader you know you are, the leader you've been all along. You know, the leader in the office who gets first pick on key projects, becomes the go-to for stakeholder presentations, is widely respected in the office, and has a presence that is not only felt but known and acknowledged.

For the record, I believe that every professional has the potential to be a leader in his or her role. Being a leader has much less to do with a title and more to do with the influence you bring to the workplace. In any role you occupy, you can position yourself as a leader. I really don't care about your level, whether you're an executive assistant or the director of a department, because leading is about your ability to influence and master the work you do in a way that helps you guide and empower others in the workplace. Leading does not always mean managing, either. You can lead without having a staff to instruct or supervise.

In 2011, I learned this lesson in my first role as a career development counselor. My then co-worker, now best friend, Amber, said I walked into the office on the first day like I was ready to take over. While I disagree with that statement, I will share that I was ready to build a career for myself and probably walked into my first day of work a *tinch* overzealous.

Up until that point in my career, I had a steady stream of jobs to earn money. I was about two years out of college and determined not to go back to my hometown in Connecticut and live with my parents. Hell, it's a responsible decision to reduce the financial burden of living on your own while starting your career and preparing to pay for your student loans, but for me, I had built a life in New York and wasn't ready to return to my small hometown. I was raised in a town where I was one of a handful of underrepresented minorities in the school system and one of fewer than five Black families in the town. I considered moving home to be the ultimate failure because my 20-year-old mind didn't understand how I'd be able to return to New York at a later time, so my decisions were primarily based on how much money I was able to make to remain in New York and less about the work that I was doing.

So, in 2011, when I accepted the role of career development counselor, I knew I was ready to have a career and was excited about the work. Previously, I had a string of roles that were based on the convenience of location, the prospect of being happier, or the salary. I was not making strategic decisions about my career; I was simply stumbling into jobs. Again, these were jobs, not a career. The position I held before becoming a career development counselor sparked a deeper interest in building long-term relationships with students, so working in career development was the answer for me. The work wasn't confined to a particular collegiate year; it spanned undergraduate to graduate and alumni in some institutions. Although the salary wasn't what I hoped for in that first role, I learned I would be eligible for a performance-based increase at six months due to a new process to increase base salaries across the university. I may have walked into the office as if I was overly confident, but I didn't know a single thing about career counseling.

On my first day, I wore my I-mean-business outfit and interacted with everyone in a calm but cautious manner until I figured out who was who. I mentally prepared myself on how to walk into an office where I was finally building a career versus how I walked into just another job. When walking into just another job, the focus is generally on finding out your assignments, mastering them, and getting out of the office by 5 p.m. When the goal is to build a career, you bring curiosity to the table to understand your role and the organization's needs so you can contribute in a meaningful way outside of your day-to-day assignments.

Shortly after my first day, Amber and I were asked to share an office, and we quickly became close friends. We worked hard and became team leaders based on the appointments seen in any given month, innovative programs with departments outside of our office, and overall reviews from students. We knew career development wasn't just a job for us; it was a career.

Amber had started working at the institution eight months before me and straight out of her undergraduate program. I came in with a few years of professional experience unrelated to career development, so we ended up being on the same track together. Six months into the role, the policy to obtain a salary increase was no longer in effect. To this day, I have no idea why this policy stopped. I just remember hitting the six-month mark and walking into my performance discussion feeling excited about recouping some of the money I sacrificed when I transitioned into higher education but being told that the money was no longer available. Knowing what I know now, I would have advocated for myself instead of walking away, but I didn't. Instead, I took this as a sign of workplace politics, and I let it pass.

Amber and I were promoted to senior career development counselors at the one-year mark, based upon our performance, and we received a performance-based salary increase. Given the norms in the office, these promotions and raises were common. If you performed well, you could expect to be promoted to a senior counselor within one year.

However, during my second year, things changed. During my first year, my goal was to learn the basics of career counseling, the office's norms, and lead the programming I was assigned. In the second year, we had metrics that were tracked and personal goals we needed to reach to move to the next level and ultimately be promoted to assistant directors. During the second year, the performance discussion with my supervisor changed how I thought about the world of work. I was in the early stages of this career path, but I was devoted and outperformed the other senior counselors in the office. I was also working on completing my master's degree in the evenings and required internships in the morning before work. At that time, I also didn't know very much about standing up for myself in the workplace, so when I disagreed with something, I'd vent to Amber, we'd grab a drink at one of our favorite restaurants after work, and I'd let it go.

By mid-2013, when my second annual review came around, I expected another performance-based salary increase and title change. I had surpassed all established goals, created innovative programs, presented at a state-level conference, and joined the board for a professional organization. Maybe you can guess how this story unfolds.

I didn't get the full increase or title change.

My supervisor believed I could have exceeded my goals far past the level I reached.

To this day, I remember my exact feelings when I walked out of his office. My mind focused on one thought – *I exceeded my goals for the year, but I could have exceeded them more*. I tried to rationalize that thought but was overwhelmed with emotion. Then, more thoughts swirled around my mind.

Did he have a personal issue with me?

Could I have done more?

Was it a race thing?

Was it a gender thing?

Why was my standard of performance different from other senior counselors in the office?

I will never know the answers to those questions, but I will always remember the feeling of hopelessness. I felt like the only option I had was to accept the partial performance increase, sit down, and shut up. I was just getting into a groove in career development and did not have any mentors to contact. I also didn't have a clue about my professional brand and how I should promote myself to other universities if I wanted another job. All I knew was that I never wanted to feel like this again.

I vowed never to allow myself to be in that position again. I never wanted to feel like I *had* to accept something I disagreed with when it came to my ability to grow and excel. I also knew I needed to better understand how to articulate my feelings in the office and back them up with facts. That day I didn't receive the raise I wanted, but that moment certainly raised the stakes in pursuit of my own personal and professional development. As a result of my experiences, this book offers the specific tactics I learned, created, tested, and implemented to attain several dream jobs throughout my career (and even a few dream offers I turned down, too).

I want you to do more than read this book. I want you to beat up the pages – highlight passages, take notes, and reread chapters. Most of all, I want you to implement what you read. You can read all the lessons you want, and you can take notes of the advice I provide, but if you don't put action behind this advice, you are essentially holding yourself back from greatness, the greatness you and I both know you possess.

When I coach clients who are uninterested in changing their ways, I remind them that they are where they are because they keep doing the same mess that hasn't worked for them. This rebellious behavior comes in many forms – using the same, tired resume, attending networking events and not talking to anyone new, and submitting lots of job applications that never make their way to a hiring manager because they were using the wish-and-a-prayer method versus truly advocating for themselves. If you are tired of doing the same things and not reaping results, it's time for you to let go of what you assumed was necessary to get a new job or position yourself as a leader and try something new, such as considering the methods I teach in this book (since you already invested in working with me by reading this introduction!).

I ask that you give this information a go. In the same way that you cannot attempt five different diet plans simultaneously and not get confused, I ask that you commit to the framework I'm sharing with you without peppering in advice from your friends, parents, and other influences. If you want to apply industry-based information, do that, but if it's someone else's opinion, let's leave that at the door for a bit. Deal? We need to ensure that your mind is clear and focused as you gear up to make stronger, wiser decisions. It's time to trust yourself.

Now, let's get ready to make your next move your best move.

To ensure you're crystal clear on your next steps, I created a section at the end of each chapter called "Your Next Move." This section is a brief recap of the chapter to ensure you know what you need to do after each specific chapter. There may be a summary of the key points to remember, or there will be specific questions for you to answer. I may even have some homework for you to do. The time has come to welcome a new opportunity to learn and grow!

You will also notice *italicized sentences* that I would like you to pay specific attention to. These are key. Again, I want you to pull the critical pieces you need to make your next move your best move. Like reading articles online where they notate how many other readers have highlighted a particular quote, the italicized sentences in this book will indicate takeaways for you, too. I am a combination of a storyteller and straight talker, so both elements are showcased in this book for your reading pleasure. Some of this information and guidance may snatch your edges from time to time, too.

I also want to acknowledge that you may not want to read this whole book right now if you know you're overdue to make your next career transition. It's really hard to think about navigating your next career move when you're in your current environment with your fair share of commitments, stress, current workload, and strong desire to leave right now.

I encourage you to allow yourself to take a step back in order to take a more confident step forward. Understanding where you are and where you've come from is key to knowing where you're trying to go next. In today's world, it can seem like we all need to know our next move at a moment's notice. But in order to do that, you have to spend time reflecting on what makes you happy, energized, and motivated to be your best self in the workplace. I truly believe that most professionals can find a job. Now they may not like that job, but there is a job to be found if times got tough. However, finding a career takes a deeper level of reflection.

While you're reading this book, take a moment to ask yourself questions that will help hone in on what you're looking for. I'll offer lots of suggestions in the Your Next Move sections, but don't hesitate to incorporate a few of your own, such as:

- When you think about your entire career, what are you most proud of?
- What are the commonalities about the jobs you really enjoyed?
- What are the commonalities about the jobs you didn't like?
- What type of support do you need from your manager and peers?
- What are the top three adjectives you use to describe your ideal workplace and company?

All of these questions will help you get one step closer to figuring out your next move. Some answers will stay the same, and many will change over time. This book is here for you to revisit as you continue to make transitions throughout your career because what you need right now will most likely not be what you need two to three years from now. In the same way there are metaphors about making friends for a particular season of your life, your career works the same way. You may stumble upon a company that was perfect for you as you learned how to become a great manager through leading project based assignments, but once you've learned all that you needed to learn, that season will come to an end. In order to continue to grow and evolve, your next season needs to include a company that will allow you to manage a team directly. The original company may have that opportunity for you, or you may need to change departments or move to a new opportunity outside of the company.

There is no right or wrong next move as long as you're strategic and intentional about what you need in your next season. In many of the later chapters, I also start to talk about incorporating feedback. Many of us may incorporate feedback when making big life decisions from our friends, family, and mentors, so why should our career be any different? I'll be with you on every page of this book, but if you're not a coaching client of mine, there are going to be professionals whom it would be helpful for you to call when you have a great interview and want to strategize on next steps. They're also going to be people you call when you don't get the job and need a boost of encouragement or help staying focused on your goal.

The reality is that you may not get every job you apply to. In this book, I even share one of the most painful job searches I've ever experienced. Just because I'm a "career and leadership" expert doesn't mean I've landed every job that I've applied for. Years ago, there weren't as many resources, career coaches, experts, or even just information floating around on the Internet to help you – but luckily, things have dramatically changed. I'm very proud to add this book that you're holding to that library of resources available to help you take your career to the next level.

We're almost to Chapter 1, but allow me to share this last piece of information with you first: In the beginning of my career, I never caught onto the subtle hints about career tactics that I overheard in conversations or read in biographies from leaders I respected. I felt inspired by their words, yet I remained unclear about what to do next. Well, I don't want you just to be inspired and motivated after reading this book. I want you to spring into action to change the trajectory of your career.

The time is now!

Part One

You must get clear on where you are coming from before you decide where you are going.

Chapter 1

Serving as a People Leader Is a Privilege, Not a Rite of Passage

Career Affirmation: I will lead my team in the way I would like to be led.

When I started writing this book, I envisioned writing my next book solely about managing people. However, it is especially important to include information in this book about becoming a people leader or currently serving as a people leader because your management experience can be an overlay to your entire career. *Sadly, in most professionals' careers, management opportunities have become a rite of passage instead of an intentional move.* When you do great work, you get more responsibilities. To manage more responsibilities, frequently you must manage people to get all the work done. In many organizations, upward mobility may be dependent upon managing people, but one of the biggest pieces of feedback I hear from clients seeking more senior-level roles that involve managing people is that they do not have management experience. It's a vicious catch-22. The only thing that makes this worse is that managers who have never had a great manager model positive behavior can become terrible managers.

Throughout my career, I've taken the most pride in being a people leader. No matter the individual tasks I have been charged with, executing them with precision has never been a concern for me. Despite managing priorities, tight deadlines, and sometimes conflicting information, I know that I can deliver impactful work. However, nothing has given me more joy than developing talent.

Doing your job is what you have been hired to do; leading people is a form of art in the workplace. As a manager, it is my duty to ensure that the professionals who report to me execute their assignments at a high level and that I prepare them for their next role inside or outside the company. It is mismanagement to ignore that there is a next step for everyone on your team after their current role. Whether that person desires to be in their manager's role or another role at the company, it's important to prioritize his or her development and the day-to-day assignments he or she must complete.

When I spoke with my husband about adding this content to the book, he asked me if I have ever had a great manager. If I am brutally honest, the answer would be that I have only had one.

I have had several bad managers, one or two good managers, but only one I would consider great. At that time, *great* meant that I felt protected in the workplace. The whole notion of needing protection in the workplace is an indication of a toxic work environment, but at the time, this particular manager advocated for fair practices for our team, stood up to senior leadership that constantly devalued the work of employees, brainstormed solutions to complex problems, and fostered an environment in which the team would be able to disagree openly but respecting other team members during tough conversations was always top of mind. My ideas of what a great manager is have continuously evolved since that role early in my career, but I define a great manager by the following behaviors:

- Creating dedicated time on a weekly or biweekly basis to discuss my work, receive feedback, and remove roadblocks preventing me from executing at the highest level.
- Advocating for me and my work when I am not in the room.
- Regularly engaging in career development conversations (outside of weekly/biweekly check-ins).
- Providing consistent feedback on my work performance with specific examples to highlight where better decisions or a higher quality of work could have been produced.
- Providing detailed, written feedback in mid-year and end-of-year performance reviews.
- Creating an environment that fosters collaboration and healthy competition among all team members.
- Fostering a working relationship that allows for co-creation of ideas, strategies, and joint execution, when possible.
- Providing radical transparency, when possible.
- Allowing me to shine brightly without reservations about my work potentially outshining theirs.

Some will look at this list and say that it is too much weight to put on a manager, but that is why I believe management is a privilege. *People leaders need to be held to a higher standard due to the increased responsibility of managing a team.* This alone has encouraged me to learn as much as possible about becoming a great manager to anyone who reports to me in the workplace and my company.

During my time in higher education, I always had a small but mighty team to execute various initiatives in the office. My teams consisted of work-study students, graduate students, workforces for specific projects, part-time employees, and full-time employees. When working in an industry with notoriously small budgets, I quickly learned to do the most with the least, including managing small teams to get the work completed.

In one of my interview processes for a full-time candidate, I vividly remember the day she walked into my office to have her one-on-one interview with me. I am known for having white-boards in my office to map out upcoming projects or systems, and my whiteboard was covered in notes and a mockup of how I wanted my team to run. I was in an inaugural role, so it was crucial that I created a roadmap for my team so we had something to anchor ourselves toward. After interviewing several candidates, I had gotten used to people being immediately intimidated by my whiteboard. While my handwriting was neat, it was filled with ideas, processes, goals, and potential key performance indicators. It was a lot of information, but I knew I needed to get it out of my head to create a plan that was ready to execute once I had a team.

This candidate walked into my office, and she understood the method to my madness that I had mapped out on my whiteboard. After we went through a few of the traditional interview questions, I walked her through my vision on the whiteboard, and she jumped right into the conversation with excitement. Most importantly, I saw that she was excited about working on a team where we would co-create new solutions to existing problems that had never been solved. She enjoyed working in a white space where the role had a lot of room to grow and evolve versus being contained to a job description that was a bit ambiguous in the first place because the work had never been done. After several rounds of interviews, she joined my team.

Looking back, I was never concerned in our professional relationship about her ability to do her job and execute on a high level. She took on every task thrown her way and improved upon it well past my expectations. We got to the point where she would solve problems without me having to ask. Since I was never concerned about the work, I turned my attention to her overall development as a professional in the workplace.

In speaking with her references toward the end of her interview process, they all confirmed that she was known for making herself indispensable to whatever team she worked on. You could tell that she took pride in not only the work her name was attached to but that she wanted to drive results in a meaningful way. Again, her performing well in her role was never an issue; in fact, I learned that I needed to proactively manage her workload to ensure that she did not take on too much work outside of the assignments she got directly from me or created for herself. I know that any manager reading this would agree that she was the dream employee.

However, what I did uncover is that I had an opportunity to work on her personal development as it related to her unique skill set in the workplace. *When someone is known for driving execution in any arena, he or she can quickly become a generalist versus a specialist.* Unless you are a project manager or chief of staff, this may not be a great trait to possess. A generalist can do just about anything, which can make it hard to brand yourself in the workplace for more senior-level roles. As you grow in your career, it is important to have "a thing," something you are known for doing well outside of task execution. Again, task execution is your job – it is the reason you get a paycheck each month! Becoming a specialist means there is a reason to hire you over another professional when there are two candidates for a role because you have an edge. You have something unique, a refined approach, a special experience that makes you uniquely qualified; you are not just another "hardworking employee" applying for a job.

During our weekly one-on-one sessions, I started asking more in-depth career-related questions to better understand where she wanted to go in her career. I asked questions like:

- *Are you interested in growing your career in higher education?*
- *Is career services the only office you would like to work in?*
- *Would you like to prepare for a role like mine?*
- *What other industries are you curious about?*
- *When are you generally ready to move on after being in a role for a certain amount of time?*
- *When you think about your day-to-day work, what are you the most uncomfortable with?*
- *What types of tasks and projects are you great at, but would prefer not to be responsible for?*
- *What types of tasks and projects do you enjoy most (regardless of your level of proficiency)?*
- *What skills do you feel like you need to build?*
- *How do you envision I could assist you in getting to the next level in your career?*
- *Is there anyone I can introduce you to in my network to assist with your career exploration or development?*

As a manager, my goal was to create a safe environment for her to explore where she would like to go in the workplace while working on high-visibility projects and leaning into the tasks and projects she enjoyed most. This is not to say I never assigned projects that she was not excited about; it is much more about awareness. *When you know your direct reports, you can create an environment where they can thrive.* In the same way married couples joke and say, "happy wife, happy life," happy employees are more productive and loyal and they have higher rates of overall work satisfaction. Even the highest-performing employees will leave a company when they do not have a positive rapport with their direct manager.

Over time, we tackled the questions I listed above and moved toward working on more developmental goals like public speaking, building strategic plans for our areas of focus, leading a technology buildout, and ultimately positioning her to move into my role once I moved on from the institution. We created an unofficial career development plan with milestones, key tasks, and long-term goals. Sure, we had a mid-year and end-of-year document that was more formal from the institution, but with high performers, there is only so much you can incorporate into that document when the focus is task execution like most performance reviews.

The plan developed through our conversations because we developed a rapport and outlined the end goal for her career. Now, if you are reading this, you may wonder what advice you should be taking from this story if you are not currently managing people. Your goal may simply be to transition into a role where you can ask some of the questions I listed earlier. However, the key to this story is that my unofficial career development plan worked so well for my direct report because she managed up, and I managed down.

In the workforce, we have been trained to think that managing down is the only way people leadership occurs. A senior-level person is responsible for creating the plan and mobilizing the work of a less senior colleague. However, managing up is just as important. Unless you are the founder, chief executive officer, the board of directors, and the client all at the same time, there will always be someone to "report to" in the workplace. The only way you can opt out of some type of managing is by being independently wealthy and not needing to work at all.

It is important to stop looking at your manager as the person who has the ultimate power in the workplace because all managers have flaws. You must advocate for yourself in this workplace relationship to ensure that your professional needs are met. Managing up is the process of managing your manager. *While the manager may be in the position of power, managing up is key to ensure that you are an active participant in creating a mutually beneficial relationship and receiving what you need most in the workplace.* If I had not asked my direct report the questions I listed, she could also have asked similar questions of me to ensure that her professional development was top of mind. She could have asked questions like:

- *What types of career development opportunities are available to me in this company?*
- *Based on my past experiences and current role, what do you feel would be my next step in this company or industry?*
- *What skills do you feel that I need to build to do my job even better?*
- *What relationships do you feel would be helpful for me to build at this company?*
- *Is there a required "time-in-role" for transitioning into my next role here?*
- *Is there anyone you can introduce me to in your network to assist with my career exploration or development?*

You are capable of initiating career conversations with your manager to ensure that you are in charge of your own personal and professional development.

Additionally, for many managers who fall into the bad or good category versus great managers, there may be something they need to see from you to help correct their negative behaviors. Unless they are ill-equipped to be a manager and found themselves in this role through their contribution to the workforce and managing was simply a rite of passage versus a piece of their developmental journey in the workforce that they were equally excited about, change can happen. You cannot help someone who is just a "bad apple." Just like romantic relationships, the person must want to change behaviors that hurt his or her partner. The same goes for the workplace.

When managing up, it is important to notate the specific moments when managers exhibit less desirable behaviors. A few common examples are:

- When assignments are submitted and there are avoidable errors
- During weekly one-on-ones where they desire more information

- When they are stressed about presenting to their manager about the information you are responsible for submitting in advance
- When they do not have enough information and must circle back to get up to speed
- When they are receiving constructive feedback about their team's work by more senior leadership and your work was called out for needing improvement

Those are just a few common examples that you may be able to identify to preemptively plan to create a more favorable experience. For example, in the scenarios that allude to not having enough information, how can you share more information before it is needed? Often, managers labeled as micromanagers desire more information because they have found themselves in situations with leadership where they could not accurately share what was needed.

There are bad managers, good managers, and great managers. Great managers ensure that developing their team is a part of their professional development plan, even if it's just ensuring that their team members have a clear succession plan when they move onto other roles inside or outside the company. And bad managers are never a reason to halt your career development plan. That is the reason I wrote this book. *You and only you can be responsible for your career movement or lack thereof.*

If you have an amazing manager, that is incredible! You are extremely fortunate. But suppose you have a manager who gives you nightmares. Well, in that case, you will need to take an active part in finding mentors, coaches, and sponsors (see Chapter 6, "Relationships Are Still Everything") who will provide you with the support you will need that you are currently not receiving.

Remember, a bad manager does not make or break your career. In the same way you are in any given role for a specific season of your tenure in the workplace, you will only have that manager during that season. And if the current situation is unbearable – well, that may be a sign to consider whether your next move will be to another department or external to your current company (see Chapter 12, "How to Know When It's Time to Go").

Management is only a piece of your career and leadership development.

Your Next Move

This chapter is one of the few chapters where I would like you to simply take a moment to reflect on your current manager relationships and determine how you need to manage up and manage down to better align with your career goals. As you begin to create your career strategy in this book, how you manage yourself and others will be an element of your plan that will take careful consideration.

After spending so many years in the career development space, I have learned that it's very hard to serve as a great manager if you cannot manage your own career well. Additionally, if you have never had a great manager and have not had the opportunity to learn best practices on leading a team, it's very hard to serve as a great leader.

If you are currently a manager, once you have your own strategy in place, you will be able to manage and mobilize your team to align with your goals and the goals of the organization. You will understand not only the end goal for your team, but also how each person plays a vital part in the long-term vision. Moreover, you'll support your team members in reaching the milestones for the team and have the strategic vision to help them create their own career development plan. Sure, you'll read this book to understand how you create your own career strategy, but great managers will be able to apply this information to empower individuals on their teams, too.

If you are an individual contributor reading this book and you don't currently manage a team, this context will help you manage your career and articulate your needs to your manager when you need to manage up. Most importantly, when the interview question comes up asking you about the type of people leader you will be, you will have the information needed to answer that question expertly.

Chapter 2

Taking Stock of Your Experiences

Career Affirmation: My past experiences support my next, best move.

After college, I was convinced that my career would look like Shanté Smith's in the film *Two Can Play That Game* (2001). I remembered Shanté's character as a high-powered executive who was confident, bold, and in control of her career. In the film's opening scene, wearing a yellow power suit, she was in her office that overlooked the city. It looked like that traditional corner office on the top floor of a corporate building that signaled to everyone in the room that "she made it."

Rather than get caught up in the relationship drama of the movie's plot, I paid attention to the snippets when she was coming to and from work, interacting with her assistant who kept her on schedule every day or speaking about the high-profile projects she was working on and how she had a tight deadline. In the film, Shanté's rival, Conny Spalding, was also a high-powered executive in the advertising space. To this day, I remember the scene when Conny, wearing a red power suit, walked up to Shanté's boyfriend's job for a meeting right after Shanté had left his office. Conny tossed her high ponytail over her shoulder and sashayed into his office building. In my mind, I imagined another scene before this red-power-suit scene, and that scene would have gone something like this:

Conny would have left her corner office on the executive leadership floor of the building in a midtown location in Atlanta or New York City, an office that overlooked the entire city with an unobstructed view like Shanté's. She also had an assistant who sat directly in front of her office, monitored her calls, kept her on schedule, and was the keeper of all her secrets. Conny's job was to make revenue-generating decisions and lead a large team of professionals who executed her vision with precision and the resources needed to work effectively. Her assistant did her best to support her and make sure she was never overbooked, received the backstory before each client meeting, and had time to eat throughout the day.

Although the film never showed any of this on-screen for either character, that is what I envisioned. Shanté and Conny were my versions of Carrie Bradshaw – driven, successful, and stylish. Mind you, I didn't have a clue how old they were or what their lives were like before this film, but for some reason, their characters stayed with me for years. Now, I'm fully aware that Shanté and Conny were grown women, not recent graduates, who probably had their own versions of professional trials and tribulations before having their corner offices. Still, back then, I wasn't thinking about the backstory. In 2008, I had graduated one year early from undergrad, and I was far from where I thought I would be after college. I received a Bachelor of Science in business administration with a concentration in marketing. Coincidentally, both Shanté and Conny worked in advertising, so I believed we were all aligned.

However, during my undergrad years, I had dreamed of internships at the top companies in New York City. Still, I ended up keeping an internship at a local publishing company in Long Island because it was one of the few internships that paid $10 per hour.

Was I bored out of my mind most days?

Yes, but I felt like it was a good decision because this internship was paid, my boss was extremely flexible, and the company had an amazing restaurant that had "high-end" French fries with over 30 different dipping sauces that I loved. *This was one of the first "mistakes" I made in my career – staying complacent and not pushing myself to get comfortable with being uncomfortable.* I was too comfortable with my easy internship and French fries to challenge myself by seeking new opportunities.

During my time in college, I was also involved in a long list of clubs and organizations. I believed my resume looked strong. I served as a resident assistant, coordinated events with the Black Student Union, co-founded a club that supported student-athletes at games, and secured one of the most coveted work-study jobs at the athletic center that afforded me the opportunity to spend my summers in the dorms for free. I was doing my best to be a great student, remain involved on campus, and earn money to support myself. When I needed more money in my pocket, mainly to save for an apartment after college, I worked at a nearby chain restaurant as a server.

When I graduated, I was excited (like most graduates), but I also felt behind. I didn't have a top internship that pipelined talent for full-time positions. I honestly did not know this was such a big thing until I later worked in career development.

I didn't have a network to contact, either.

I still had to take one more science class to technically graduate in three years instead of four, and I knew I wanted to stay in New York and not move home to Connecticut.

I had work to do.

My internship at the local publishing company offered me a full-time job after graduation, but I knew that wasn't going to be "it" for me. In my eyes, that was the backup plan until I secured a full-time role or postgraduate internship that aligned with my Shanté and Conny dreams. In short, I had to find my way to land a job in New York City.

I attended university career fairs and worked with my career services office. However, I was still missing several solid career strategy elements and had no clue how to launch a robust job search that aligned with my interests, goals, and an empty wallet. Really, my priority was making money so I could stay in New York. After some quick research, I learned that living in New York City wasn't going to be an option due to finances, but I knew I had to at least stay in Long Island after college.

Luckily, I was able to stay in the dorms throughout the summer after graduation, so during that time, I took my final science class and worked at the publishing company, the chain restaurant, and the university athletic center. I had to save as much money as possible to apply for an apartment and pay two months' security deposit and the first month's rent. I saved about $3,000, the most I ever saved on my own. With all the hours I was working and a little help from a refund check from the student loan I needed for my summer class, I was on my way to living my post-graduation dreams.

As I moved into my first apartment, which left a lot to be desired, I remained nervous about my job situation. Amid anxiously applying and waiting to hear back from a potential employer, one of my cousins reached out to me to see how life after graduation was going. He was a salesman at a New York City-based office supply company. I mentioned that I was on the job hunt, and he graciously introduced me to the owner of the company, which led to my job as a marketing analyst.

The Importance of Self-Assessment

Becoming a marketing analyst may seem like my dream just occurred, but it didn't. This company chose me. I didn't choose it. They essentially needed an entry-level professional to do some work, and I was an entry-level professional who needed work. I had no idea about my personal brand and how to articulate that during an ambiguous introduction. So I received a role that was as ambiguous as I was about my skill set. I had no leverage when negotiating my salary and benefits, and that's how I landed my first role out of college, making $25,000 per year with no benefits for the first 90 days. Oh, and marketing analyst was the "fancy" title I was given to cover up that this was really a data entry role. Apparently, the company assigned me this title to sweeten the deal and align with my degree. My main responsibility was updating the pricing on various products that customers would order. That was my job in a nutshell. My salary wasn't paying all my bills, so I continued to work at the local chain restaurant on the weekends to make ends meet. Despite this undesirable turn of events, I was in New York and remained committed to finding my way. In hindsight, I wish I had learned about self-assessment.

I have a picture of me and my parents from a Student Affairs award ceremony in 2008, right before my graduation, and I always reflect on how clueless I was during that time. I was beaming with pride, which is understandable. After all, I was about to graduate from college, which is a feat in itself, but I was naive about my next steps. At that time, the only thing I was thinking about was making money, and if I'm brutally honest, I barely knew how much money I needed to make to survive on more than cereal and tuna fish sandwiches.

Reflecting on that time, I could have opted to take a career assessment like the Myers-Briggs Type Indicator (MBTI) or Gallup's StrengthsFinder. These assessments would have indicated something about how I experienced the world, my strengths and needs in the workplace, but I needed to dig deeper into my experiences to understand what I had to offer to the world.

Fast-forward to today, my clients often come to me to gain a deeper understanding of themselves and interpretation of their strengths and opportunities after taking an assessment. *However, I always reinforce the importance of looking deeper into yourself and past experiences to make informed decisions versus praying that your next steps will be determined by a test or survey.* I prefer clients to complete a simple exercise that allows them to dissect the skills they've acquired from each role and determine which skills they'd like to continue to use and which skills they would like to stop using. This brief self-assessment exercise helps my clients determine their skill set and allows them to use this information as they begin to communicate who they are as professionals. We will touch on this more in the "Your Next Move" section at the end of this chapter.

Let's circle back to my "marketing analyst" job. From day one, I knew I wouldn't last very long at the office supply company. I was miserable, and the office was far from my New York City and Shanté and Conny dreams, so I began reaching out to a few of my classmates to see what everyone else was doing. Some folks were happy; others hadn't found anything, and some found jobs like mine where they were grateful to be paid but were unhappy. Since I graduated a year early, many of my original classmates were still in college, wrapping up their last year. In the eyes of those friends, I felt like the one who "made it out" that needed to share that they had to do everything they could before graduating to make sure they set themselves up for success. I had spent so much time working in a comfortable internship and participating in many extracurricular activities that I forgot to think about life after college versus the fairy tale version I envisioned.

In one of these conversations, I connected with Dave, a former classmate whose wife worked in financial services. I never saw myself as a personal banker, but after a few conversations, I felt like banking was something I could do, and there was also a clear career path I could embark upon if I loved my experience. The office supply company was a family business, and it was clear that promotional opportunities were not available for me. Even if I returned to the publishing company, which was also a much smaller, family-owned business, my growth and internal mobility options would still be limited. Dave worked at the same company as his wife and was wildly successful. Years after our conversation, he even went on to become one of the nation's top 100 personal bankers. If he was able to graduate college and become successful in this role, I knew I'd be able to as well. This felt like my first intentional career decision where I'd grow and excel if I enjoyed the opportunity. Although there are many studies about professionals, and not just millennials, rarely having 5-, 10-, 15-, and 20-year careers at the same company, I was still hoping to find this opportunity.

The realities of the work world are that most college graduates will not land their dream role and stay there until retirement. That's just not how the world of work operates. I'm the daughter of a Sergeant E-5 Army veteran and retired postmaster of Waterford, Connecticut. My dad has a history of landing a position and working his way up from the bottom. This instilled the notion that I must work my way up from the bottom, too. All I needed was a chance to get into a role, and I told myself that I'd be able to work my way up into any role I desired if I played my cards right. Although I never envisioned building a career in banking, I told myself I could make something out of this opportunity. At the time, a good career opportunity was tied to longevity and a career progression plan. I wanted to walk into a role where the next role was clear. I saw so many professionals get into jobs and then have to figure it all out once they were settled in the role, but I wanted something more defined. I wanted a role where there was a set of options available if I was successful. I wanted to see a desirable next step. This has been a common theme throughout my career.

I've told every manager I've had that seeing the "next step" keeps me motivated and inspired to do my work. It's not that I need a timeline to get there. I just desire to know there is a next step for me, pending excellent performance and time in the role.

In my first role out of college as a marketing analyst, it became clear there wasn't a "next step" for me. There was not another marketing role in the company at the time, and I wasn't interested in moving into another department. In hindsight, I didn't even know that understanding there was a "next step" was something I desired – until I didn't have one. The personal banker job looked like the perfect opportunity for me to hit the reset button on my career and restart in a role that would support my career for years to come.

The Value of Transferable Skills

Dave's wife put in a referral for me, and after several rounds of interviews, I landed the job. Although I wasn't familiar with the financial services industry at the time, I had learned more about how to leverage my existing skill set to position myself for the role versus hoping the company would know I was a decent worker. Dave and his wife helped me match my existing skills as a marketing analyst to the role of a banker, so I'd be able to articulate my value throughout the interview process.

At the time, it felt like I finally had a cohesive story that explained my transition from college to my first role and then hopefully to the personal banker role. *However, now I understand that this way of speaking was simply a way to highlight my transferable skills to a future employer. I learned how to pull out the skills I obtained in that first role and apply them to a personal banker's role.* By the time I went into the final round of interviews with the district manager, I had connected all of my skills to the role so well that I was confident my days spent looking at office supply data would be numbered. Matched with the referral from an accomplished professional within the bank, I was able to get my foot in the door and restart my career as a banker before needing to sign up for benefits at the 90-day mark at the office supply company.

Following my acceptance of the role, I went through three months of training to obtain my financial services and insurance licenses. I felt like I was back in college because new hires started together and generally studied together daily until everyone obtained their licenses. This was the experience I needed because it almost felt like I could "go back to college" since we were studying for seven hours a day. I had been so unhappy in my first job that I was excited to be back in an environment that felt like a classroom again. Studying for my Series 6 and 63, and Life and Health Licenses wasn't easy since I've never been great at standardized tests, but I was excited when I passed each exam on the first try and was assigned to my first of two branch locations.

I spent nearly two years as a personal banker and quickly learned that the role was less about connecting clients with recommended products and services, and much more about hitting my quotas to keep my job. This was my first experience with a sales role, and I wasn't a fan. I loved getting to know my clientele, helping them with their finances, and connecting them with other services that the branch offered, but the pressure to sell was too heavy. To make matters worse, I worked in a high-net-worth area in Long Island, so it was hard to get "quick wins" like credit cards or new bank accounts, at least for me.

Once I realized that this wasn't the career path I wanted to embark upon, I went back to the drawing board to assess the transferable skills I collected during my time as a personal banker and how I could use them moving forward. Looking back, this is where I learned how to break down transferable skills without someone guiding me through the process. I needed to figure out how to package my current skill set to work in a new environment that didn't necessarily look like where I was coming from. Since I had nearly three years of professional experience by this time, I knew *intentionality would be key in moving into a role where I would be happy*.

Know When It's Time to Go

Let's break down this concept a bit more because once I understood the value of communicating my transferable skills in my career, I was set. At the time, I worked in financial sales and realized this wasn't the place for me. I had acquired the skills of quickly taking in new information, building and maintaining client relationships, and matching client needs with products and services. The last time I remembered being happy was in higher education, so I thought I should consider working in higher education versus simply being a student. Still, I knew I would have to articulate in interviews how my career was spent at an office supply company and in financial services.

This is the type of career transition that most professionals assume is the norm – switching from one industry to another unrelated industry. Intuitively, I knew I needed to find a way to speak about my experiences but relate those experiences to the new industry and the role I was seeking. Again, self-assessment came into play to highlight the transferable skills I gained in banking and apply them to higher education. In interviews, instead of speaking about the day-to-day logistics and tasks of my work, I focused on the larger themes that would be more applicable to other roles. Knowing this, I scrubbed all the industry-specific information out of my resume. I focused on the skills, not tasks, that would be easily recognizable to whoever would be interviewing me.

In this process, I quickly realized that while I did not like selling, I could apply my skill set to another sales-like job, such as serving as an admissions counselor. The role of an admissions counselor is understanding the university (quickly taking in new information); building relationships with students, families, and guidance counselors (building and maintaining client relationships); and helping students determine which educational and extracurricular programs align with their interests (matching needs with products and services). I couldn't just walk into an interview and speak about my Series 6 and 63, and Life and Health licenses; focus on the high-net-worth clients I served and how I helped them apply for mortgages; or how I worked with an investment officer. That wouldn't make sense to whoever interviewed me if they had never worked in the financial services industry.

Once I made these changes to my resume and made mental notes to adjust my verbiage in interviews and follow-up career conversations, the interview requests started to roll in. Although I was not offered the first few jobs I interviewed for, I connected with an opportunity and was eventually hired. I received an offer letter within 24 hours of interviewing with the hiring manager and a key stakeholder. At this time, I still wasn't truly clear on what I was doing with my career, but I knew I wanted to be happier. *In hindsight, moving with intentionality and seeking happiness were the first strategic career moves I ever made.*

It's also important to note that I took a $20,000+ pay cut when moving from financial services to higher education at this point in my career story. One of the most common questions I'm asked when professionals look to transfer to a new industry is if it's worth it to take a pay cut. I knew I was taking a pay cut to be happy, and if I continued to grow my career in higher education, I would make up the deficit as I continued to grow and learn. *If there is a vision for how a move will impact your career trajectory for the better, then taking a temporary pay cut is okay if your livelihood isn't affected.*

I will never advocate for accepting a salary that doesn't allow you to make ends meet, but if you can cut back and feel happier while making less money, the transition may be worth it. For me, the salary reduction was well worth it! I remained in an affordable apartment, cut my cable, and budgeted carefully to ensure I would not overspend.

Did I want more during that time?

Of course, but I knew the temporary reduction in expenses would pay off in the long run.

Your Next Move

In this chapter, I shared personal stories about some of my first career moves and how I slowly but surely learned how to advocate for myself once I understood how my past experiences made me uniquely qualified for various jobs. Most importantly, I briefly covered how to assess yourself to understand your skill set by using a quick activity, the importance of transferable skills, and walking away from an opportunity to intentionally pursue opportunities that will make you happier. I will never advocate walking away from a job and figuring it out as you go, but I'm big on leaving jobs where you are unhappy and realize the role is not a good match for your skill set. In this chapter, I also mentioned that I would circle back to explain a simple exercise to assess your skill set. So, let's break that down:

On a piece of paper, write every job you've held. For recent graduates, this can include part-time roles and internships. For experienced professionals, your list would include all the positions you would highlight on a LinkedIn profile or resume. Next to each position, write every skill you acquired from each role. Last, highlight the skills you would like to continue using and cross off the skills you would like to avoid using moving forward in your career. For example:

Role/Company	Skills Acquired
Marketing Analyst at Office Supply Company	Customer service; data management; relationship building
Personal Banker at Financial Services Company	Quickly learns new information; builds client relationships; matches needs with products and services; selling products and services
Assistant Director of Admissions at a College	Student-centered approach; building and conducting presentations; succession planning

Now it's your turn. You will most likely need additional space, so feel free to grab a notebook to draw this chart and list all the important jobs you've held in your career (you can go to nextmovebestmovebook.com to download an editable version). After completing the chart, answer the following questions:

1. What are the top skills you've acquired throughout your career?
   a. What skills do you consider your strengths?
   b. What skills helped you obtain the greatest results?
   c. What skills do you find yourself teaching others?
2. Moving forward in your career, what skills do you prefer not to use?
3. What skills do you want to use in your next role, company, or venture?

After answering those questions, you should have a clear list of your transferable skills that you would like to continue to use in your career. The self-assessment exercise is simple, so simple that it would be easy for you to skip because you feel like you already know your skill set, you've been in the game for a while, or you're looking for advanced strategies. *However, I encourage you to do this exercise because if you cannot quickly showcase your skill set in career-related conversations, you are at risk for presenting yourself as a Jack or Jill of all trades and a master of none.* Associating yourself with keywords like hardworking, a perfectionist, and a great team player is great, but those words apply to nearly every professional in the workplace who cares about his or her performance on the job. When someone speaks about you or your career, you want to be associated with skills and not colorful adjectives.

Also, when I refer to career conversations, I'm not just speaking about when you're looking for a job or a performance conversation with your manager. *Every conversation with a professional who has the potential to influence your career is a career conversation, and those conversations are important to showcase and reinforce your skill set. You need to get comfortable with unapologetically sharing the gifts you've acquired from your experience in the workforce with anyone who will listen.* Speaking about your skill set is not bragging. You are sharing your gifts to achieve the mission and vision of the company and your personal goals. Not every manager will recognize and reward you for the skills you're using and acquiring in the workforce, and that's okay! However, that makes it even more important for you to get comfortable sharing these skills in your conversations, so you're not unintentionally playing small and not setting yourself up for future career opportunities.

Regarding transferable skills, this is more about moving from Point A to Point B in your career. Like many professionals, you will most likely make a few career changes. Hell, you probably made quite a few before you picked up this book! *It's your job to connect the dots when having career conversations. It is not the interviewer's job to figure out what you're truly good at and why you made certain career moves.* The interviewers' job is not to decipher the jobs you've had on your resume to determine how you're the best fit for the role they are interviewing you for. If you are applying to internal roles at your existing company, your potential new hiring manager's job also does not include determining that you're ready for the next role, even if it's lateral.

All of that is *your* job.

I frequently use the phrase "create a career that creates opportunities for itself," but I realize that many professionals do not fully understand what that means. Whether you're conscious of this or not, you are creating your next steps based on your workplace experiences. As you build a career, skill sets, relationships, degrees, and other experiences, you create potential opportunities. *Each time you make a move in your career, you are taking part in creating that opportunity for yourself based on what you've done up to that point. You just need to be comfortable connecting those dots to the next role.*

Part Two

Evaluate your past experiences to understand where you want to go.

Chapter 3

Core Values Are the Essence of What Make You Happy

Career Affirmation: I am attracting a workplace that aligns with my core values.

henever I interact with current students, undergraduate or graduate, I always share that internships are
beneficial for two main reasons:

1. Internships confirm you are on the right track of applying
   your academic knowledge to the workplace because you
   enjoy your experience.
2. Internships confirm that the hands-on experience you're
   gaining is not a great fit and you may need to go back to the
   drawing board in the classroom or try a different work setting next semester.

The same is true of any work environment, role, and company,
even if you are no longer a student. Each experience will teach you
something about yourself, and it's okay when something isn't the
"best fit."

During my time as a personal banker, I quickly learned what
"sparked joy" and what did not. During the three-plus months of
training with aspiring bankers, I enjoyed the camaraderie of the
training environment in a remote office location in Long Island,
New York. We buckled down in the training center and studied for
our financial services licenses for seven hours a day. We had a strict
hour for lunch, and then we went right back to hitting the books.
In hindsight, this was like a college environment but with a much
more regimented schedule. I recall studying daily with Jose and a
group of two other potential bankers. Each day, we arrived at the
training center and manually signed in by a certain time. Lateness
upon arrival and returning late from lunch were not allowed. At
the end of each week, we had a training test we had to pass. Failure
resulted in losing the opportunity to be placed as a banker. The
room was filled with 40 to 60 potential bankers, but we lost a few
each week.

This period was stressful, but the relationships, camaraderie,
and structure were enjoyable. Everyone with the same start date
was working toward a common goal. We had to go through the

same process to reach the same outcome, passing our Series 6 and 63, and Life and Health licenses. Despite my disdain for standardized tests, I was passing each exam on the first try.

I still recall when potential bankers would get called into a small office inside of the larger classroom. If you got called into the office, it generally wasn't for good news. You'd see potential bankers being called into the room, in the corner of the study room farthest from the door, to receive the news that they were no longer able to continue studying for their licenses, essentially losing the personal banker job before they even got into a branch, having to do the "walk of shame" to the other side of the room to grab their belongings and head out the door. Oddly enough, despite some of those terrible circumstances, I thrived on the camaraderie and structure that was created, and I consider Jose a friend to this day. In fact, I called him to ensure I included the correct details from our studying days in this chapter.

Once we transitioned into branch locations from the training center after passing the required tests, the atmosphere significantly changed. We had new managers and new teams, and we were the newbies at our respective branches across Long Island, New York. Our small group was reunited a few times during the first six months for additional training classes, but we were no longer a team. Moreover, the focus was no longer a communal goal; it was an individual goal closely tied to individual performance and pay. Ultimately, the goal was tied to my livelihood. If you hit your sales numbers each month, you were in the clear. Too many months of not hitting your sales goals and you were put on a performance plan, and your employment would be terminated if improvements were not made.

I quickly learned that I loved interacting with my clients, learning about their lives and how their finances tied into that. I can still recall the financial advice I received from some of my wealthiest clients and how that advice continues to impact my life and financial goals to ensure that I can take care of myself and the people I love. One of my largest clients had over $14 million in liquid assets at the bank. I had never seen this type of money in an account. I remember being unsure if I was saying the correct numbers when quoting her balances. Each time she came to the branch, she would come to my desk, and we would do an overview of her accounts, but I also learned about her family, children, and views on money. She always advised me to "have my own money," no matter my relationship status. Even though I was a banker and was supposed to be advising her on financial products, she shared some of her best and worst financial decisions and different options she used to save money for her children's college tuitions, even though they were far from college age.

Another client had noticed a change in the interest that her account was earning, and while my manager wanted me to have the client call customer service, I sat with her and went line by line in her account until we realized what had happened. While this took over an hour of work when I was supposed to be "selling," we bonded, and I also learned to look at my accounts in greater detail.

My client relationships were great but what began to frustrate me was the lack of camaraderie and the push to sell. I began to experience fellow bankers stealing clients while I was on my lunch break or vacation. While the team generally knew which clients belonged to which banker, leaders considered clients fair game if a banker was on vacation and there weren't copious notes on exact client conversations. I vividly remember the day I came back from vacation and one of my clients needed help with her account. Another banker sold the client a product that resulted in a large commission. From the moment I walked into the branch location, that banker avoided me because he knew I would find out about the sale and try to argue commission credits with the branch manager since the client was mine and I had already put notes about potential opportunities with the client, although I had yet to close the deal.

I also remember when my numbers were low for the month, so the branch manager was pushing for me to "work the lobby," which was a way of asking bankers to approach customers as they entered the branch locations and speak with them before they reached the tellers to process their transactions. The goal was to contact the customers, help them process their transactions, and get to know more about their financial situations to recommend potential products or services that would result in commission. After working the lobby without much success, the branch manager asked me to begin making cold calls to potential customers assigned to me in the system, but after a few minutes, the manager came back and asked why I wasn't working in the lobby.

Y'all, I felt like I was losing it!

I was already frustrated from feeling the pressure of not hitting my sales targets, and now I was being asked to work the lobby and make sales calls at the same time. Clearly, that was not possible, and I promptly addressed this with the branch manager.

"You asked me to work in the lobby, and I did that. Then, you asked me to make cold calls, and I started doing that. Now, you're asking why I'm not working the lobby. I can't do two things at once. Which one would you like me to do?"

Seeing that I was frustrated, the branch manager called me into their office to talk, and shortly after that, I had the opportunity to transfer to a branch location closer to my apartment. I jumped at the chance. However, the new branch location didn't turn out to be much better. I ended up loving my new managers, but it wasn't the environment I was seeking. This was the first time I inadvertently learned about my working core values. I thrive in environments where I feel that the department or team is working toward a common goal. In other words, I look for environments with strong camaraderie built into the day-to-day work in the role, similar to the training experience I had when I started in financial services. However, I was in an environment where every man was for himself, and the only goal was to stay off the radar for underperforming, so you didn't end up on a performance improvement plan. What's more, we were often pressured to sell products and services to potential and current clients to ensure we hit our sales goals. It was understood that we must look for every potential product for the client to hit sales goals, and the branch held us accountable for having those conversations no matter how well we knew the client.

When one of the district managers would visit our branch, they would sit in on conversations we would have with our regular clients. Generally, personal bankers did not have private offices, so managers would simply "linger" near your desk to eavesdrop on conversations so they could provide feedback after the client left. It didn't matter if you saw the client the day before or knew their financial history inside and out because the district manager wanted us to go through a script with the client to ensure no opportunity was left on the table. Some clients understood what was happening and "played the game," while others got frustrated, and it would ultimately damage the relationship. It didn't matter what I wanted to do, though, because I had to follow the script to keep my job.

In this environment, I quickly learned that although I loved building relationships with clients and their families, I had no interest in following a sales script to get a sale to reach my goals, which was really about not being put on a performance improvement plan. What made me love the job were the authentic relationships I built with clients, the lessons I learned about financial management, and the problems I could solve to improve financial situations or fix an issue with client accounts, all of which had no bearing on my commission. Circling back to my core values, relationship building is extremely important to me.

I desire to build close relationships in every experience. *Close* doesn't have to be synonymous with *best friends*. For me, *close* means being understood, connecting on a professional level, and working collaboratively from a place of mutual respect or toward common goals. I knew my time in financial services would come to an end because of not having genuine relationships and a collaborative spirit in my environment and work tasks.

In the strangest turn of events in my career, I was in a car accident while heading home from work, about 20 minutes from my branch location. I was rear-ended on 495 in Long Island, New York. I was safe, but the accident affected my back and neck. My doctors recommended I take sick leave from my job to recuperate and seek care from a neurologist. During this time, I also made sure to apply to a few jobs and leverage my transferable skills to make a career transition to higher education.

Shortly after returning from sick leave, I was able to interview and secure a role that I felt was the best move to better align with my core values. This was one step closer to my first dream job as a career development counselor; I just didn't know it at the time. I wanted to be back in higher education, and I found a role as the assistant director of admissions for a mid-size college not too far from my home. This role allowed me to leverage my sales skills in a new environment where I believed more in the "product." In this role, the product was education, and that's something I will always believe in. This role not only spoke to my skills in relationship building, but it aligned with my core values as an individual and as a professional. *Core values are the essence of what makes someone happy, so if you can align your core values with your career, you will maintain a level of happiness in your day-to-day work.*

We spend 40 hours per week working (or more), so it's crucial to have a sense of happiness and fulfillment. Regardless, when you know your career goals and strategy, you're able to tell the difference between an opportunity that aligns with the next steps you'd like to take in your career and just another job opportunity. Knowing this difference allows you to continue to create experiences that align with your core values, so there's some level of satisfaction, thus making the role much better than just another opportunity you're simply falling into.

Every time I've been ready to make a career move, I was so ready to make the transition that any new opportunity sounded perfect, and any extra work I was asked to do in my current role felt like I was wasting time. Every extra moment I had was consumed with identifying new opportunities, seeing if I had existing relationships that would give me a better chance at being called by a recruiter, and ultimately interviewing or presenting at companies to help secure the role. I never looked into my personal or working core values because my only goal was to get a new job. In my transition from financial services to higher education, I was more strategic because I knew I wanted to return to higher education, but I lacked clarity on which role or department would be the right fit. At this time, I just knew the move made sense, and I could easily explain my rationale in an interview. I leaned on knowing that once I made the transition, I would have time to figure it out and learn more about the different departments in a college from first-hand experience, rather than from interviewing professionals in my network or asking for introductions to second-degree contacts of professionals already in my network. This is where my career strategy stopped.

"Get in and figure it all out." Period. That was my motto during this time.

But *"get in and figure it all out" is not a strategy; it's an escape plan. If you want to build a career and ensure your next move is your best move, you must be strategic.* The best analogy I use with clients is to think about that friend in your life who is constantly in and out of relationships. This friend breaks up with a partner on Friday, only to have a new one by Monday. While his ability to remain open and in search of love may be inspiring, we could also argue that this person may need to hit the time-out button to assess why he is constantly in and out of relationships, especially if his goal is to be in a long-term relationship that leads to marriage.

I was doing the same thing with jobs, escaping one bad role for a potentially better role. If the grass looked moderately greener, I was down to give it a go. You never want to recycle jobs like old romantic partners. *You need to be intentional to ensure you select jobs that align with your core values so you actually create a career versus a string of experiences that will never add up to having a career you'll love.* While you may understand what type of role you want, can you identify what makes you happy at work, what values to look for in a manager, and what values to look for in a company? Most importantly, you must understand the values that are important to you so you can identify what works best for you within the confines of a company. I was clueless yet grateful to transition to higher education before I ended up on a dreaded performance plan and was forced to end my career as a personal banker.

Your Next Move

It's time for you to understand your working core values. Before we speak about developing your career strategy, it's essential to understand your core values so you can identify opportunities that align with your values. One of the quickest ways to uncover your working core values is to think about some of your greatest accomplishments and "do-better" moments. Do-better moments could be described as failures, but I like to call them do-better moments because most of the time you can easily identify the actions you could have taken to do better. Write your three greatest accomplishments on a sheet of paper and your three do-better moments. Identify the common themes among them. For example:

Accomplishment: Finishing my master's degree program one semester early while working full-time.

Do-better moment: Not advocating for myself after being denied the promotion to associate director.

Common themes: Accomplishments, recognition, and upward mobility.

The common themes generally turn out to be your core values. Don't worry about making your accomplishments and do-better moments related or exact experiences from the same job or company when doing this exercise. Write the top three experiences or situations that come to your mind and identify the common themes.

If you have trouble identifying your core values, use the following list of common core values to help you determine which of them most closely align to your greatest accomplishments and do-better moments you just listed.

Accessibility	Collaboration	Diligence
Accomplishment	Comfort	Discipline
Accountability	Commitment	Diversity
Accuracy	Communication	Drive
Achievement	Community	Eagerness
Adaptability	Competence	Education
Adventure	Competition	Effectiveness
Affective	Comprehensive	Efficiency
Agility	Confidence	Empathy
Aggressiveness	Connection	Endurance
Alertness	Consistency	Energy
Altruism	Continuity	Enthusiasm
Ambition	Contribution	Entrepreneurship
Appreciation	Control	Equitable
Approachability	Cooperation	Excellence
Assertiveness	Courage	Fairness
Awareness	Courtesy	Family
Balance	Craftsmanship	Flexibility
Belonging	Creativity	Focus
Boldness	Credibility	Freedom
Brilliance	Curiosity	Fun
Calmness	Customer Focus	Generosity
Capability	Daring	Global
Caring	Decency	Gratitude
Certainty	Decisiveness	Happiness
Challenge	Dedication	Hard Work
Change	Democratic	Harmony
Character	Dependability	Honesty
Charity	Determination	Hospitality
Cheerful	Development	Humility

Humor	Personal Development	Results
Impact	Personal Growth	Risk
Independence	Persuasive	Sacrifice
Individuality	Philanthropy	Safety
Innovation	Power	Self Awareness
Integrity	Precision	Simplicity
Knowledge	Proactive	Stability
Leadership	Productivity	Structure
Longevity	Professionalism	Success
Mastery	Profitability	Support
Merit	Prosperity	Systemization
Meticulous	Punctuality	Teamwork
Mindful	Pursuit	Training
Modesty	Quality	Transparency
Open-Minded	Recognition	Trust
Optimism	Reflection	Uniqueness
Order	Relationships	Vision
Originality	Resilience	Wealth
Partnership	Resourcefulness	Willfulness
Passion	Respect	Winning
Performance	Responsibility	Wisdom
Perseverance	Responsiveness	Work/Life Balance

Source: Adapted from https://www.threadsculture.com/core-values-examples.

As we get closer to assembling your personal career strategy document, you'll be including these core values as a reminder of what feels best to you in the workplace. Again, we spend 40 hours (or more) per week working, so it's crucial you're in alignment with your core values on a regular basis. Whether you're looking to get promoted or take a power lateral role, your core values will serve as an anchor so you're able to easily accept or reject opportunities that are not congruent with your career strategy.

If you'd like to get a head start on your career strategy document, feel free to flip to the end of Chapter 13 or you can go to nextmovebestmovebook.com to download an editable copy of the template that will allow you to add also fill in your core values right now.

Chapter 4

Setting Long-Term and Short-Term Career Goals

Career Affirmation: I am positioning myself to become a leader in my industry.

In Chapter 2, I shared that I imagined myself graduating and becoming the modern-day version of Shanté Smith and Conny Spalding in *Two Can Play That Game* (2001). When this film came out, I was still in high school, and I never saw it at the movie theater, despite the film opening at No. 2 in the United States during its first weekend. When I learned about this film, it quickly became a favorite in my DVD collection.

Two Can Play That Game has absolutely nothing to do with career and leadership development, yet these two characters impressed me. Ironically, the film does not show many scenes of the characters doing any work, except an event that Conny organized. However, that scene still focused on the relationship plot of the movie. But, I wasn't paying attention to the relationship drama during the film. To this day, I don't know why these characters made such an impression on me. I was a marketing major in college when I watched this movie, so I frequently dreamed of getting to the same place in my career as Shanté or Conny, but I had no idea what it would take to get there. In fact, it wasn't until I was 10-plus years out of college that I started to think about how old Shanté and Conny must have been in that film. After I rewatched the film to make sure I had the storyline correct for this book, I noticed there is a quick one-liner in which Shanté reveals that she is only 28 years old. So, no matter what I did, I had an unrealistic expectation at 21 years old.

What I recognize now is that this was one of the first times I had seen Black women in influential leadership positions in corporate America. My bookshelf has always been filled with books on Black history, so I had no shortage of inspiration about successful Black professionals in a variety of industries, but I'm assuming that I was simply young, impressionable, and desiring a "sexy career," and Shanté and Conny had that experience in the film.

Knowing this, I stress that having a long-term career vision to focus on is great, but I work with clients to ensure they have a clear, attainable, short-term vision based upon where they are today. *While the long-term vision is a great goal to look toward, the short-term vision is also what keeps you motivated on a day-to-day basis.*

Adults commonly ask children what they want to be when they grow up, but it's rare to see that same adult break down the steps to reach that profession. Adults quickly share a smile or follow-up questions on why children are interested in certain careers. Doctors and lawyers bring smiles, and "less profitable" careers have follow-up questions, right? When we watch fiction movies like *Two Can Play That Game*, we see a snapshot of a time in a character's life. Depending on the plot, that snapshot can be a day, month, a few years, or a lifetime, but the film only shows a snapshot, not a play-by-play, that a bystander can quickly implement to achieve similar results.

No matter what I did, it would have been impossible to have a Shanté- or Conny-like career upon graduation because I had no clue what I would have to do to get there. After building a career in higher education in the career-services department, I became well-versed in advising students and alumni on almost every career path, but there is nothing like a first-hand account of the daily nuances in any career. *Having candid conversations with professionals doing the work, participating in internships and postgraduate rotational programs, and working in the industry are the only ways to understand if a particular career is a great fit for you, and even as we think about long-term goals, I always share that long-term goals are a moving target.* As you grow in your career and skill set, your long-term goal can quickly shift as you obtain new skills, experiences, and opportunities. Often, we focus on the end goal instead of the series of steps (short-term goals) to get there.

It wasn't until my fourth professional job that I had a long-term goal to work toward. After a few months in my role as a career development counselor, I was excited to explore the profession and truly understand what it would take to progress and become a director of career services in a college or university setting. In my experience, directors of career services departments have spent much of their careers in the industry and have held various positions inside career services offices and academic advising. Once they received the director position, they were pretty much set to sit in that role for the remainder of their careers unless they aspired to serve as a dean or provost. I loved the feeling of a director role being a place where I would have the opportunity to settle in and have longevity, like my dad's career and career services directors across the country. It was not uncommon to see a director stay in that role for 10, 15, or even 20 years at the same university! Many would return to school after receiving a master's degree to pursue a doctoral degree and later be elevated to higher-level positions in the university. I finally felt excited about my career path.

Looking back at all the jobs I've held in the span of my career, I'm always surprised at how things shifted. Now, I can easily tell the story about why I made each move and how those moves help me today, but in my first few roles outside of my undergraduate studies, I took many leaps of faith, hoping to have a fulfilling career I could be proud to hold.

If I'm brutally honest about each move in my career, I wasn't strategic until my first career development role. Each decision to move into a new role "felt" better because I was excited to explore a new role or industry, but it wasn't a strategic move. It was honestly an escape from one role to another that I only hoped would be better than the last. When I moved into career development, I was finally in a role that I was excited to build a career in. It's hard to be strategic about your career when you are unsure of the industry you're working in and have no idea what that career would look like long term. I knew that career development was a field in which I would be able to make a significant impact once I learned the ropes. Plus, at the time, the university I worked for aligned with my core values. In the early days of my first career development role, my issue was simply a knowledge and experience gap that I was quickly able to fill.

I remember shadowing a series of career coaching sessions with undergraduate students. I watched my manager conduct the sessions and then we spoke about what I learned in a debrief session at the end of the day. After one of the sessions was over, I looked at my manager and asked, "How do you know all of this information about different types of careers?" That day, I watched at least four career coaching sessions with students having completely different career paths, and he always had the answer. He knew exactly what resources to provide the student, and I was excitedly taking notes on places he mentioned to create a list of resources to email the students later that day and save as a point of reference for myself. I was amazed but quickly learned that he was once in my shoes. About 15-plus years prior, he felt clueless, nervous, and uninformed to speak to students, but with experience came knowledge. That day, I began paying more attention to short-term goals to build my career versus only focusing on the long-term vision. Although I could not stop thinking about when I would be able to serve as a director of career services, I needed to focus on the exact steps I'd have to take to get there.

Long-term vision reinforces a destination to reach, and that destination is a moving target as you grow and gain new experiences. *Therefore, short-term goals are even more important. Short-term goals create milestones for you to accomplish that will lead you to your long-term vision.* You can use those career milestones to check in with yourself to determine if you are still aligned with your long-term vision regularly. If you find yourself out of alignment, you can determine whether the long-term vision must change or if you need to get back on track and reassess your short-term goals.

Figuring Out Where You Are Now

Before we get into determining your next move for this chapter, it's important to figure out where you are right now, so you have a baseline for your goals and overall career strategy. I have four key designations I share with my clients in one of my signature group coaching programs and one-on-one leadership coaching sessions. Every goal or milestone we create for their career strategy begins with where they are at that moment.

Right Role, Right Time

In this designation, there is generally room for you to grow in your current role because:

- Time in the role is 18 months (or less).
- You do not fully understand how your role fits within the greater vision for your department or company.
- You do not have strong relationships and advocacy for your work.

Right Role, New Skills

In this designation, you are seeking additional responsibilities in your current role because:

- Time in the role is 12 to 24 months.
- You fully understand how your role fits within the greater vision for your department or company.
- You are starting to establish and maintain strong relationships and support for your work among stakeholders.

New Role, New Skills

In this designation, you are seeking a new, most likely lateral role to grow your skill set with expanded responsibilities:

- Time in the role is 18-plus months.
- You fully mastered your current role but acknowledge there are skill gaps that need to be addressed before going into a promotional opportunity.
- You have strong relationships and support for your work among stakeholders.

New Role, New Experience

In this designation, you are seeking a promotional opportunity because:

- Time in the role is over two years.
- You have fully mastered your role and developed a cross-functional skill set.
- You understand the larger strategy of the department and company.
- You have strong relationships, advocacy, and sponsorship for your work.

Where do you see yourself based on those designations? Although most professionals immediately jump to "New Role, New Experience" based upon not wanting to be in their current role, I encourage you to think about your current skill set and if you've truly mastered and created an impact in your current role. Would you be ready for the next level if the opportunity arose? There is nothing wrong with a stretch assignment or a lateral opportunity because you want to learn a new skill before jumping to the next promotional opportunity inside or outside of your current company.

When I have career conversations with my direct reports who are eager to move into new roles, I always ask them to evaluate their impact versus their "time-in-role." Many times, we look at "time-in-role" as the indicator of when it's time to move on, but that's literally only a measurement of how long you've physically been in a given role. Many organizations indicate that they like to see less senior colleagues move into new roles at around the two-year mark, but what happens if you haven't made an impact as yet?

Moving for the sake of moving is never your next, best move. While each forward move you make needs to be strategic, you also need to consider the impact or legacy you're leaving behind. For example, if your current role is brand-new to the organization and you were charged with mapping out the strategic plan for this new team and role, you may need more than two years in the role. Year

1 was most likely building the roadmap, gaining buy-in from stake-holders, hiring a team, and then executing a strategic plan. Year 2 is focused on fine-tuning the strategic plan and potentially scaling or cutting back in key areas. By year 3, there are most likely still more ways to create impact or improve upon existing processes to cement your legacy in this new role.

At this time, you may not have even had the opportunity to get bored because you're building the train tracks while the train is still moving. You have to execute the work to solve problems while you're still building the strategy! In roles like this, you may not hit "New Role, New Experience" until you're three to five years into the role. Moreover, impact is tied to a level of completion as well. If you were to walk away from that role today, how would you describe your impact? Did you see a process through from begin-ning to end? Were you able to innovate and improve upon the initial strategic plan so moving forward you've already experienced alternative ways of solving a problem?

If you are in a position where you had a successor who built a clear roadmap for your job and your sole responsibility was to con-tinue to execute the work your predecessor was doing, two years in that role may be more than enough. You were likely challenged in your first year as you navigated the various seasons of the role, but by year 2, you may be twiddling your thumbs if there aren't opportunities to innovate in your role. Your only goal in this type of role was to master a defined skill set; once you've mastered the skill, your time is up! Your impact here is defined by your ability to keep the train moving on the tracks that your predecessor built.

We will talk about this more in Chapter 11, "The Truth about Salary Negotiation," but it's important to note that impact and results drive your salary conversations as well. If you've been in a role and you can articulate your impact and results as they relate to the role you're interviewing for, that helps to showcase the value you bring to the workforce. For example, take the first example I shared earlier for the professional who is brand-new to the organi-zation and charged with mapping out the strategic plan for a new team and role. In year 1, the roadmap will most likely be built, the team is onboarded, and in the first phase of execution. If that leader were to leave for the sake of leaving, that work will be incomplete. The impact will be incomplete because full execution was not possible in one year. Additionally, if the person was leveraging this inaugural role to move into another similar role at another company, what happens when he or she hits the one-year mark at the new company and is having to troubleshoot their strategy?

If that professional had committed to the process of driving results and creating an impact, he or she may have been able to proactively improve upon the roadmap earlier on at the new company. I know some professionals may not care, especially if that new company is paying more money for the same work, but here's a little food for thought. If you are able to execute a plan, acquire new skills, and create an impact in your current role, how will that help you move smarter and faster in your next role?

Your Next Move

It's time to start thinking about setting short-term and long-term goals for your career. People love to set fitness goals, relationship goals, and other goals, but many times, career goals merely remain a vision. We have a "final destination" in mind that we hope to reach but don't have a clear idea of the experiences we need to take our careers to the next level.

Some of us have a vision board that appears to be an exact vision of what success in your career would look like. On one of my old vision boards, I would have pictures of executives at board tables and cutouts of 30-under-30 or 40-under-40 awards. I even used to host vision board parties to share my specific board creation process because I believed in the process so much! Over time, I learned that the board could give many people a false sense of accomplishment since there is no plan behind a pretty vision board with pictures and motivational words. *The power of a vision board, or vision of success in your mind, is in the plan with specific steps to make the vision come to reality.*

For those who have no idea about their long-term vision, that's okay! If you haven't experienced a position that makes you feel excited to wake up in the morning and log in for work, you need to evaluate the experiences that would allow you to explore the skills you would like to acquire while you figure out your next steps.

In my line of work, many professionals have stated that their company helps with career development planning, and I always push back to share that the planning your company provides is not enough. Most companies will only prepare you for lateral or promotional opportunities at that company. A company will rarely invest in your personal and professional development, fully acknowledging that your next career move may not be at that company, especially if there is no benefit to them. That is why you need to have your own career development strategy that consists of short-term and long-term goals that will serve as milestones for your career.

In this chapter, I've shared that a long-term vision is a moving target, but before we get into short-term goals, we need to check-in and determine what your ideal day would look like in five years. I promise that the long-term vision will change several times in your career, and you will be responsible for updating your career strategy, but we need a destination to help anchor your plan. When you think about where you are in your career, I want you to envision where you would like to see yourself in the next five years. Ask yourself the following questions:

- *What time would you wake up for work?*
- *Where is the office located (virtual or in-person)?*
- *Describe your leadership team.*
- *Are you a manager or an individual contributor?*
- *Do you work in teams or solo?*
- *What types of projects are you leading?*
- *What are the expectations of your role?*

- *How much influence do you have in important decisions regarding your team or company?*
- *What are the core values of your company?*
- *What is the trajectory for someone in a role like yours?*
- *What is the title of the role you would like to occupy?*
- *How do you feel walking into or logging into work each day?*
- *What time do you leave or log off from the office each day?*
- *Are there any special perks in the role or company you are interested in?*
- *What are the names of the companies you would be interested in working for?*

Those are a handful of questions to consider when thinking about where you would like to be in five years. While answering those questions, please jot down anything else that comes to mind that you know is important to the role, company, culture, or environment you would like to work in.

Once we know where you see yourself in five years, it's important to work backwards to create a clear strategy to get you to that five-year vision based on the designation you feel fits where you are today. I recommend working in three- to six-month blocks to understand the milestones you would need to hit to reach your five-year vision. We will cover building your career strategy more in Chapter 7.

As you're fine-tuning your long-term vision, I also encourage you to think big. Many times we focus on the vision that we feel is attainable instead of the vision we'd actually like to achieve. Sure, you may think, and even intuitively know, that landing a vice president role when you're currently a senior manager isn't realistic in five years, but if that's what you really want to do, then let's build a plan to get there. One of my business coaches drills home that when your vision isn't big enough, your execution won't be either. Essentially, when you set small goals, you make small efforts because you know "you'll get there." It's too easy not to. However, when you have a bigger vision, you know you have to show up every single day to ensure you are taking action to reach your destination. Even if you don't reach the larger long-term vision, you'll end up much further along than you would if you only worked toward a smaller long-term vision.

Right now, it's important to note that as you read this book, you will learn about additional piece of information you'll need to incorporate into your strategy that will all come together in Chapter 13, "Putting It All Together," or in the career strategy template that you can download at nextmovebestmovebook.com. Your strategy, milestones, tasks, and subgoals will not be complete by the end of this chapter. As we dig deeper into where you are right now and where your gaps are, I encourage you to revisit your strategy document and add any new information. You will also check in with this document at least once a quarter to ensure you're on target and make changes as needed. Remember, your long-term vision is a moving target. You may also have an experience that radically alters where you would like to take your career. Better yet, maybe you will cultivate a great mentor or sponsor who assists in expediting your career strategy. You must leave room for the unexpected.

Years ago, I had a business coach who would help me set monthly, quarterly, and yearly goals, and once the document was finished, she always encouraged me to leave room for abundance. On the document, I would physically leave a space and label it "abundance." As wonderful as it would be for every industry to have a dedicated career path that everyone could follow with flawless execution, that's just not how the world of work operates. When building out your short-term goals, I encourage you to facilitate informational interviews with professionals who are currently in positions similar to those you would like to see for yourself in five years. Understand the paths they took to get exactly where they are now. If you do not have relationships with anyone in the roles you're interested in, Chapter 6 will be crucial for you as you begin to navigate your career. You can also use LinkedIn to review the backgrounds of professionals in these roles. Ensure that you notate the following:

- *What skills did they acquire? In what roles did they acquire those skills?*
- *What educational and workforce experiences do they have (different companies, the same company for an extended time, and certain degrees)?*
- *Did they have managerial experience before this role?*
- *What did they feel was the most important thing they had to do to acquire their current role?*
- *Are they involved in any professional organizations?*

Once I realized that my long-term goal was to obtain a director of career services role in 5 to 10 years, I conducted informational interviews and a lot of LinkedIn research to analyze the careers of directors in colleges and universities where I'd like to work. I noticed the following:

- Most directors had built a career that included backgrounds in human resources, talent acquisition, student development, career services, academic affairs, and student affairs. Although it was common for them to "work their way up" in one office, adding new skills with each role, I also saw current directors who changed universities to get into higher-level positions and gain new skills and promotional opportunities.
- At a minimum, most directors had a master's degree, and many were working toward doctoral degrees in education, too. As each professional increased the level of his or her role, each ended up staying longer in that role.
- Managerial experiences began for most professionals once they landed assistant or associate director-level positions.
- Regarding the professionals I spoke with, they noted that understanding the demographic of the students they worked with was particularly important. If they started their career outside higher education, it was clear that they leveraged their industry experience to work with students or had volunteer or

relevant experience through external organizations that helped them land their role in career development.

- Once professionals began to dig deeper into their roles, they frequently joined related local-, regional-, and national-level professional associations.

Now, it's your turn:

- *What skills did the professionals in your field of interest acquire? In what roles did they acquire those skills?*
- *What educational and workforce experiences do they have (different companies, the same company for an extended time, and certain degrees)?*
- *Did they have managerial experience before this role?*
- *What did they feel was the most important thing they had to do to acquire their current role?*
- *Are they involved in any professional organizations?*

In the next chapter, we will dig into the gap between where you are now and where you would like to be.

Chapter 5

Addressing Where You Are, So You Are Ready for Where You Want to Go

Career Affirmation: I am capable of bridging the gap between where I am and where I would like to be.

After you are more clear on your short-term and long-term goals, the next step is addressing any gaps in your career. While I'm on the subject of gaps, let me clarify that I'm referring to the literal gaps in knowledge, experiences, and relationships that need to be addressed to take the next step in your career. This step is even more important if you see yourself in the "Right Role, Right Time" or "Right Role, New Skills" designations shared in Chapter 4.

One of the biggest misconceptions when building your career strategy is that you will naturally get to your desired destination with time. Time is not the only gap between where you are and where you'd like to be. Early in my career, I had the mentality of working hard and staying the course. Both of my parents had careers in which they stayed in a role for 10 years or more with the mindset of working hard and doing great work. Dad would always tell me to do the following:

1. Work hard and focus on being the best at whatever you do.
2. Excellence is always important; be excellent.
3. If they hit you first, hit back.

Knowing these principles, I've always strived for the next level, excellence, and a new level of perfection. As a seasoned professional, I can now build a career based on my strengths. I've held enough roles to identify how I would like to spend my days in the office and what skills I'd like to continue to build upon and magnify in my work. However, as an entry-level and confused midlevel professional, I needed to understand my gaps in knowledge, experience, and relationships that would take my career to the next level. It's not that I needed to downplay my strengths, but to get closer to my long-term goals I had to acknowledge the gaps so I could attack them.

You may find yourself working hard throughout your career but not "moving the needle" far enough to help you get into the next role. You may even ask your manager for feedback, and he or she can share that you're doing great and encourage you to keep up the good work, but there is no constructive feedback to help you improve and be considered for higher-level roles. *Spending significant time in a particular role does not always make you qualified for a lateral or promotional role. There is a gap between any two roles that must be bridged with knowledge, experience, and relationships. Often, it's up to you to figure out what that looks like for you.*

In the Introduction, I shared the story of the performance discussion with a supervisor that changed how I thought about the world of work. After one year of working in the position, I received glowing remarks and the full performance-based salary increase. However, two years later, after surpassing established goals, creating new innovative programs, and building cross-departmental relationships (while pursuing my master's degree and completing a mandatory internship), I did not receive the full increase during that performance appraisal process. At that time, I had no outside connections, an unpolished and unrecognized professional brand, and was clueless about what it would take to never be in that position again.

While I could easily focus on the circumstances or reasons that my manager did not recommend me for the full performance-based salary increase, I want to turn your attention to my feeling of hopelessness. There have always been inequities in the workplace, and when they occur, you have three choices:

1. Do nothing.
2. Remain at the company and fight for what you believe is right.
3. Apply to roles in other departments, companies, or industries that better align with your core values and level of experience.

What many professionals fail to acknowledge is that before you apply to new roles, internal or external, there are many things you must do before transitioning into a new role. Sure, you may be able to land any old job if you need something immediately, but do you want to keep recycling jobs like old romantic partners, or do you want to build a career for yourself? If you want a career for yourself, you need to make strategic moves, but it's really difficult to be strategic if you are as hopeless as I was.

I was hopeless because I was simply "happy to be there." I finally had a job that I genuinely liked, but I felt overlooked, underappreciated, and not valued in a way that I deemed suitable based on how other professionals were being rewarded in the workplace. I remember leaving my manager's office and saying, "Thank you for your time," yet I was fuming. I began pulling the numbers of a few metrics we used to track performance, and I was always No. 1, if not No. 2, to my best friend and co-worker, Amber. I was truly conflicted on whether I should storm into my manager's office and demand stronger feedback or start hunting for another role.

Despite feeling hopeless, I chose to hunt for a new role. It's important to note here that this was a personal decision I made. In Chapter 12, I'll cover more on when it's appropriate to leave versus when it may be worth trying to stick it out. In my mind, I just heard all of the baby boomers and Generation X professionals yelling that "leaving was a very millennial thing to do," but sometimes leaving to grow is one of the best things that you can do in your career.

As I prepared to make my next career move, I realized that I had never been in a position where I liked what I was doing and simply wanted to find another lateral or promotional opportunity. So, my focus was finding an opportunity that would continue to build my career in the same industry. I also realized that I did not fully understand where I'd be "ranked" against other applicants when it came to knowledge, experience, and relationships. It's easy to look at a job description and read that the company requires two years of related experience, but I knew I had some professional gaps to understand better.

Lucky for me, one year prior, I had gotten involved with a professional organization, the New York State Cooperative and Experiential Education Association, so I had a few career development professionals I could ask for objective advice regarding what they look for in applicants to their career center, but that was about it. Even in those conversations, I acknowledged that I wasn't comfortable having this exploratory conversation with someone in a position of power who could influence my job search. Oddly enough, I had been coaching students on preparing for informational interviews and networking conversations, but I didn't have as much practical, hands-on experience in a situation that mattered to me. I loved connecting with professionals in my industry and was great at casual conversations, but I had never done this when I needed something. In Chapter 6, we dig into relationship building, but it's important to note that this was one of the personal gaps that I needed to address.

Besides relationships, from the few conversations I initiated with other career services professionals, I learned more about the structure of roles in my profession and whether I would be considered qualified for a lateral or promotional opportunity. Aside from meticulously reading the job descriptions and comparing them to my existing resume, I took a wild guess about whether I would be able to perform in the role. Since I had only been in my profession for a little over two years, I decided to apply for lateral roles in larger organizations and promotional roles in smaller organizations. Within five months, I secured a promotional opportunity at a smaller organization that was a part of a larger university network, so it felt like I had the best of both worlds. However, those five months could have been reduced to three months if I had a clearer understanding of my gaps in knowledge, experience, and relationships.

Understanding these gaps is really about your own personal and professional development. However, it's easier for many of us to understand the gaps in professional development. Once you have a career strategy in place, you have a better idea of how to stay in alignment with your strategy, provided that there aren't any surprises along the way. Oftentimes, you may spend countless hours and money for degrees, and then you continue to invest in your craft to set yourself apart as the leader in your field through certification programs or even with a mentor to better understand a particular system or project directly related to your work. For high-achieving professionals, professional development is natural because it's almost required to rise to the next level. While many of us are taught to pursue professional development, very few of us are taught the importance of personal development.

Personal development is just as significant as professional development. It's about creating a plan for who you want to be and the areas in which you want to grow as a person. Becoming a leader in the workplace isn't just about your ability to drive results; it also has a lot to do with your ability to connect, develop, and impact your company, department, and peers along the way. This means setting goals for developing the areas of your life that may not be strengths. In the same way you can identify strengths and weaknesses related to your work and create a strategy around how you can become better in these areas, the same can be done for you on a personal level. Personal development requires self-awareness. It requires you being honest about where you are while assessing where you want to be in six months, twelve months, five years, and so on. If you can't see where you are now, you won't be able to get to where you want to go. If you can pinpoint areas of opportunity, you can then incorporate these elements into your overall career strategy.

While we definitely live in the generation of YouTube University, it's still important to invest time and resources into your personal growth and development. When you make the decision to invest in yourself, it requires you to take an active part in your own growth and success, devoted to seeing an improved outcome. Investing holds you accountable for taking steps to grow. For instance, if your goal is to lose 15 pounds before the summer, paying for a trainer keeps you accountable to your personal development goal. You could stay accountable to yourself, but that doesn't always work for everyone. For many of us, at the first sign of an obstacle, we quit working toward our goals. Investing in our goals keeps us pursuing them.

An easy way to invest in your personal development is to devote time to building a relationship with someone who is a thought leader or someone who has more experience in the areas in which you desire to develop. There is something to be said about learning from someone who has put in the work to become an expert in their field. They will be able to not only share their success stories, but also to identify the obstacles they overcame in order to rise to their current level in their career. This is one of the many reasons I often speak about relationships throughout this book. In Chapter 6, we talk more about the types of relationships that are important to cultivate, but as we speak about your personal development, it's important to notate where key relationships can also help you in this department.

In the span of my own career, I've learned to seek out relationships to challenge my opinions, beliefs, and experiences for my own personal development. If we are honest here, I'm a Type A professional who hates being "called out" when I'm wrong. I take pride in getting things right the first time, and I have a long history of beating myself up for making mistakes that are easily identifiable by others, especially managers in my professional roles. However, as I've grown as a leader in professional settings, I've challenged myself to seek out professionals to provide constructive feedback about how they've experienced working with me in the office, my executive presence in meetings, perceptions about my leadership skills, and general feedback on how they feel I can further develop myself.

For many high-achieving professionals, the work is never the major point of concern. The work always gets done, right? However, there is always room for improvement on a personal level so you can prepare yourself to combat increasingly more difficult obstacles as you grow in your career. As you transition into the "Your Next Move" section of this chapter, don't forget to include both personal and professional developmental areas into your career strategy.

Your Next Move

Like Maya Angelou said, "When you know better, you do better." So, let's begin to understand your gaps concerning the five-year vision of your career. Another way of looking at this gap is to ask yourself the following three questions:

1. What knowledge do I need to acquire?
2. What experiences do I need to cultivate?
3. What relationships do I need to build?

Let's start with question 1 – What knowledge do I need to acquire?

When most professionals think about "knowledge," they immediately think about educational backgrounds. *While your educational background may be a key factor, other forms of knowledge do not always fit into the realm of receiving a particular degree to fulfill the requirements for the role.* For example:

- Knowledge of a specific subject or demographic of persons
- Knowledge of a particular technology
- Knowledge of a particular industry

Knowledge may seem the same as an experience, but I've intentionally separated the two to reinforce that "knowledge" does not have to come from an educational background or formal work experience. You can have specific knowledge from research, education, life experiences, and interests, all of which we tend to forget to incorporate when understanding our knowledge and applying to roles.

Next up is question number 2 – What experiences do I need to cultivate?

The fastest way to understand the experiences you need to acquire is by finding a few professionals in the role similar to your next logical step and conducting an analysis similar to what was mentioned in Chapter 4. The only difference is ensuring the professionals you speak to are in the next logical role for your career and not your five-year vision. You don't want to jump to your 5- or even 10-year vision if that's not your logical step, because that wouldn't help you build a plan to attack the current gap you have right now.

In your research, determine if there is a "bridge role" you need to take before you are ready or qualified for the next role. *A bridge role is a special role that would allow you to gain experience in an area that you know will provide you with the exact experience you need before moving into your career's next milestone.* Generally, this would be a lateral role or a stretch assignment focused on helping you develop a key skill or gain specific knowledge. A bridge role is also not a bad thing. In fact, many times, a bridge role is the next logical career move.

Before you become a manager, you were an analyst.

Before you become a director, you must serve as a senior manager.

Generally, there is a "chain of command," whether formal or informal. In conversations with professionals in the roles closely aligned to your five-year vision, I encourage you to notate their answers to the following questions:

- *What was your journey to get to your current position?*
- *What did you study in college? Do you have undergraduate and graduate degrees or certificates only?*
- *What types of projects are you leading?*
- *How large is the team you manage?*
- *In what area is the bulk of your experience?*
- *Were you using transferable skills to land this role, or did you have direct experience in the field?*

Once you complete your analysis, objectively compare and contrast your experiences. No two career journeys are the same because you are unique individuals, but this exercise will better inform you of the steps you may need to incorporate into your career strategy by understanding how other professionals navigate their transition to the role you are most interested in obtaining.

Now, let's approach question number 3: What relationships do I need to build?

Understanding gaps in relationships is far less black and white than understanding gaps in knowledge and experience. However, I would argue that relationships may be considered more crucial when getting ready to make a career transition. When you look at your five-year vision, I challenge you to ask yourself the following relationship-based questions:

- *Who are the key stakeholders I will be interacting with?*
- *Who will I need to work with to accomplish my day-to-day work?*
- *Who will I need as my mentor for the first 90 days in the new role?*
- *Who would be a great sponsor to get me into the next role?*
- *Who will be my new peers in the new role?*

Often, we allow ourselves to play small in our careers and we feel as though we don't belong in the room until we reach a pre-determined level or are specifically invited to have a seat at the table. So, we don't pursue the crucial types of relationships that will help in the next role. *I challenge you to start building those critical relationships before you think you need them.* Some of those key relationships would be with:

- Your hiring leader
- Your hiring leader's manager
- Your hiring leader's peers
- Your direct peers in adjacent departments
- Human resources manager assigned to your department
- Recruiter for the department you're interested in

When thinking about a career transition, the piece of advice I share most, and, essentially, the reason for writing this book, is to help you get ready before you need to be ready. *If you are waiting for the perfect opportunity to arise to start addressing the gaps in your knowledge, experiences, and relationships, you are too late.* Sure, you can continue to repeat the mantra of "what's for me will be for me" when you miss out on career opportunities that you believed you were qualified for, but have you ever thought about the reason you missed an opportunity? If you're objective, maybe the role wasn't for you because you may have been ill-prepared to work on that level, or maybe another candidate was able to secure mentorship and insider information through colleagues who currently work in that department that helped them navigate the interview process better. Again, let's get you ready to make that next career transition while you're currently excelling in your role. I don't believe in the notion of the perfect balance between any two things because that sets us up for having unrealistic expectations about those two things always operating in harmony. However, I believe in finding the time to work on two goals in tandem, especially when it comes to doing great work in your current role and addressing any gaps that will prevent you from rising to the next level in your career.

Chapter 6

Relationships Are Still Everything

Career Affirmation: I am attracting relationships that support the long-term vision for my career.

I used to be one of those people who hated networking. I thought networking was what affluent families and business owners did at the local golf club on weekends.

As for me, I had to rely on my hard work to get wherever I wanted to go, and I figured relationships wouldn't help me much. I always came back to my dad's three pieces of advice:

1. Work hard and focus on being the best at whatever you do.
2. Excellence is always important; be excellent.
3. If they hit you first, hit back.

Dad was right and wrong at the same time. I needed to do all those things, but I also needed to build relationships to support those three things at the same time.

My first professional job out of college was at a small office supply company in New York City, and I got this job because I had a cousin in the sales department who introduced me to the CEO of the company. My second job in financial services as a personal banker was attained through a referral from one of my under-graduate classmates' wife. Trust me, I could go on and on how relationships helped me, but I never thought of them as a huge contributing factor early in my career. In my mind, I was able to get into these roles because I was hardworking and interviewed well. I didn't yet understand how crucial it was to have a solid pro-fessional relationship in order to get a warm introduction to a company.

When it came to the act of networking, I thought that you would meet a new person and immediately have to ask them for something. After you introduce yourself and identify the need or desire of that person, you would begin your elevator pitch. Essentially, your elevator pitch was your only opportunity to ask for anything that you needed in that moment. That's where I was 100% wrong. Now, I view relationship building like making friends, but less personal at times.

Early on in my career, I worked under a leader who did not support my involvement with professional organizations. Still, I always advocated for attending organization events and meetings at my own expense and making up my hours outside of the office, if necessary. I was frustrated that I didn't have support from my leader. Still, I knew it was important for me to continue building my relationships inside and outside the office to increase my opportunities to be promoted in my field.

In higher education, I quickly realized it would be easier for me to move from institution to institution for promotional roles, rather than waiting for an internal promotion to the level I desired. Therefore, a large part of my career strategy was ensuring I connected with career professionals at institutions in New York and New Jersey, where I could easily commute to and from for work. In my first role in career services, I had become a member and board representative of the New York State Cooperative and Experiential Education Association (NYSCEEA), but I realized that many of the professionals in that organization were located in upstate New York. Once I secured a role and moved to New York City, I quickly refocused on building relationships in geographic areas where I could see myself working. Within a few months, I started attending events run by the Metropolitan New York College Career Planning Officers Association (MNYCCPOA) and Career Counselor Technology Forum. Again, I was unable to receive reimbursement from my employer, but I knew attending those events was crucial to my success and ability to build relationships outside of my current office.

At one of the events, I connected with a known leader in higher education. At the time, this person was a director of career services at a high-profile university and known for working in marketing and social media for career centers. With any profession, I always tell my clients there are "stars" in the profession who are known for their knowledge, innovation, and best practices. This person is one of those stars. After seeing this individual present a case study at a professional development event, I was immediately drawn to her, and I made it my goal to introduce myself before the event was over. Besides complimenting her presentation, I was at a loss for words and had no idea what else to say to make an impression, but I noticed she was wearing a structured jacket similar to the coats that Kerry Washington wore in her role as Olivia Pope in Shonda Rhimes's hit show *Scandal*. As I nervously fumbled with my introduction, I remember telling her that I loved her jacket and noted that she would probably love The Limited's *Scandal* collection. She was gracious and thanked me for the tip. I still recall that short conversation, and I kicked myself for only mustering up the strength to complement her attire, but it was a start.

That was the end of our conversation that day, but I remained engaged for the remainder of the professional development event and made an effort to keep in touch. I returned home, added her on LinkedIn with a quick link to the *Scandal* collection, and noted that I would love to keep in touch and follow her work.

For two years, I followed her work and kept in touch via LinkedIn. I did my best to follow her posts, comment when I had something to add or share, and attended events where she was speaking. I also worked on expanding my professional brand through networking with professionals in the areas I was potentially interested in working. I also pushed myself to continuously be an innovator in my work and submit topics to present at conferences, so whether I was sharing a best practice in a quick, five-minute presentation or diving deeper into a project lasting more than 60 minutes, I made sure to showcase my skills, especially when I knew she would be in attendance.

Fast-forward two years after I met her. She reached out to me on LinkedIn about a role in her office. I had never dreamed of working at the university, but through this connection, multiple rounds of interviews with stakeholders across the university, and a final presentation to a large portion of the current team, I secured the role. This was a key experience for many subsequent opportunities that came my way personally and professionally. Before my experience at the university, I hadn't worked under a leadership team that supported personal and professional development, so my experiences outside the office environment were limited to what I was able to manage on my budget.

One of the first things I wanted to do with the office's support was to connect with a professional organization that had a national audience. I wanted to learn about what was happening in my region and learn from professionals from coast to coast. I had spent my entire life and career on the East Coast, so that was all that I knew up to that point. Once I was settled in my role, one of the key experiences in my career that allowed me to understand the power of mentorship was participating in the National Association of Colleges and Employers (NACE) Leadership Advancement Program. Although the program had several components, I found the most value in the informal mentorship program. The program assigned each program participant a mentor, but it was up to the participant to build the relationship and leverage the mentor to help us in our careers. I was connected with a former president of NACE, who was, at the time, serving as the director of early careers at a Fortune 500 company. Although this individual worked in a corporate setting, as opposed to higher education, I was excited to learn about her unique perspective on my career growth and potential opportunities.

However, what I valued most outside of our candid conversations was her willingness to open her network to me. Knowing my goals at that time, she facilitated introductions to three other professionals aligned with the potential future positions I was most interested in. Extending my relationship to her network was a major game-changer. After that experience, I added a simple but impactful question to the recommended list of questions for all of my clients conducting informational interviews with potential mentors or professionals in their industry: *Is there anyone in your network that you think would be a great person for me to connect with?*

At the time, I didn't ask that question. Instead, her kindness opened those new doors for me. However, since that time, I have connected with countless professionals whom I wouldn't have otherwise met without a formal introduction into their networks, because I asked that question. *There are power players in every work environment. To get in contact with those power players, it's best to be introduced by a mutual contact or find a way to initiate a conversation through a common interest.* We all know those people who will proudly shove a business card in your hand at an event or monopolize your time at a virtual event by speaking about themselves. In those situations, you find yourself saying, "Does this person lack self-awareness? Because it feels like the air was just sucked out of the room."

I recall being at a networking event when someone shoved a business card in my hand and said, "Call me if you need help with such and such." I promptly gave them the card back. They looked shocked, but I politely explained that I don't know anything about their work, business, or why I should call them. It didn't matter if they worked in healthcare, insurance, accounting, higher education, marketing, or any other field. We didn't have a meaningful conversation that would make me want to speak with them about any of my needs, and because they quickly shoved their card in my hand and were attempting to walk away, they also had no idea what I needed either.

After that person got over the shock of me handing the card back, we ended up having a wonderful conversation about what networking really means. Networking and building relationships have nothing to do with the volume of events you attend or the number of business cards you hand out at an event. *Networking has much more to do with the relationships you can cultivate and sustain.* When I think about the relationships I previously mentioned in this chapter, both of those relationships exponentially helped my career, but my focus was singular in the beginning. I wanted to build authentic and meaningful relationships with them individually. Through my relationship with the director of career services, I was connected to a job opportunity that took my career to the next level. I know it would have been significantly harder to transition from higher education into corporate America a few years later if I hadn't worked at that university. Through my NACE mentor relationship, I was connected with other professionals who helped my career and entrepreneurial journey.

Looking at my relationships differently was a turning point in my career. The relationships I've seen yield the most results in my career were also holistic. They were not contained in the environments in which I usually met people. Instead, they spanned my personal and professional endeavors, so the relationship did not "expire" when the experience ended. Often, we look for relationships during a specific season in our careers without thinking about the support we will need in the years to come. "What got you here won't get you there" is one of my favorite quotes by Marshall Goldsmith. *We often think about our careers as unrelated, singular sprints, as if we make one career move and need to restart our strategy and erase our previous work. However, every experience you've had, good and bad, has shaped the next move in your career, and the same goes for your relationships.*

Each relationship you've cultivated does not have an expiration date. As you grow and make career moves, the people in your network are (hopefully) doing the same. As you grow and expand your skill set, experiences, and expertise, so is everyone else in your network. Continue to keep in touch with key stakeholders, regardless of your industry and current role. As you think about the culmination of attributes that make up who you are, remember that the professionals you're connecting with will be doing the same, and you never know when someone may be essential for your career.

Having worked in higher education, I am very familiar with writing letters of recommendation for my students. Whether the letter is for a scholarship program or a graduate degree program, I've written them all. Once in a while, two to three years will pass without contact, and a student will reach out in need of a letter. Two to three years in college is a very long time. Students change majors, club affiliations, and focus areas, and they can be a new person in two to three years. Without keeping in contact during this time, I always decline to write the letter of recommendation. Sure, I could write a lukewarm letter that vaguely speaks about my experiences with the student, but that wouldn't help the situation. You want your relationships to remain close, so whomever you connect with is up to date on your personal and professional experiences and can support you if and when there is an ask.

Before we transition into the "Your Next Move" segment, it's important to address being in a virtual environment. At the time of writing this book, the workplace was still a virtual environment for any company or role that was considered nonessential due to COVID-19. Many companies are having candid conversations about webinar fatigue because many employees have spent nearly a year being glued to their desk on virtual calls from 9 to 5, or sometimes longer. However, it's important to still find ways to connect and maintain relationships.

The key to maintaining relationships in this virtual environment is prioritizing the individual time and attention that would have happened in an office environment. In the office, you may have left your desk to grab a coffee after a stressful meeting and a colleague would have joined you. Or you'd take the elevator with the same person at the same time every morning and you would eventually introduce yourself and grab lunch in the office cafeteria. Leaders would walk into meetings and realize they needed one of their managers to join them to walk through a process or project they were leading. All of these interactions need to be recreated in a virtual environment to ensure that you're still making valuable connections to support your work.

Once of my biggest fears about the future of work after COVID-19 is that professionals who have not mastered how to continue to build relationships will be unable to make to their next moves with ease. Yes, the quality of the work will always be important – that's the basis for any strategic career move – but building the stakeholder advocacy, key relationships, and acquiring the insider information to position yourself comes from relationship building. It may have been easy to sit behind a desk all day and never speak to a single person while we were in the office, now that we are all in our own homes, behind screens, you can become invisible.

I encourage you to look at the ways that you would have interacted with professionals when you were in the office and find ways to recreate those same scenarios, for example:

- If a meeting ended five minutes early and you would have debriefed with a colleague, reach out and see if you can hop on a quick call.
- If you generally had a team outing on the last Friday of the month, coordinate team happy hours at that same time to celebrate the end of the workweek.
- If you would "run into" your favorite leadership team member quarterly at the business overview meeting, set a reminder on your calendar to schedule a 15- to 30-minute check-in at the same time as the business overview meetings.
- If you attended a bimonthly professional development event, ensure that you subscribe to the organization's newsletter to learn about virtual events and make a habit out of scheduling a follow-up meeting with at least one person who was at the event.
- If you know that you made most of your new relationships from referrals, reach out to your colleagues and ask for introductions to their favorite contacts in the company and set up 15- to 30-minute introductory conversations.

While these actions may be out of your comfort zone, being in a virtual environment and building key relationships will take a bit more intentionality.

Yes, everything feels so different in a virtual environment and we may all be tired of being in virtual meetings all day, but I challenge you to find a way to participate that feels good to you so you can continue to build and maintain relationships.

Your Next Move

Relationships can expedite success in your career.

That isn't to say I recommend building a relationship with anyone and everyone for the sake of knowing people, but I will share that building relationships is a crucial piece to consider when building your career strategy. The following are a few key relationships I would like you to build to support your career strategy:

1. *Peers*: In every work environment, you will have colleagues in a similar role and at the same level. Even if they are in different departments or functions, they would be considered peers. Instead of always looking up when building relationships, it's equally important to build relationships laterally. For companies with structured and thorough interview processes for managers and people leaders, the companies will most likely ask your peers if they would support being managed by you. Having great peer relationships is a great indicator of your character and leadership abilities. I always give the example of building relationships with executive assistants. Not only are these colleagues in the know about the leader they support, but they are gatekeepers. Do you want to get 15 minutes on a senior leader's calendar? Well, the executive assistant has the pull and a close relationship with the senior leader to advocate for that urgent meeting. Do you want to understand the best time of day to speak to a senior leader? The executive assistant would have that information. An executive assistant holds so much information by being close to a senior leader, even though it may appear that they are in a role that lacks seniority in an organization.

2. *Coaches*: Your first instinct may be to quickly indicate that you do not need a career coach. Although that may be your preference, you still need coaches in the workplace. A coach's responsibility is to teach you something in the workplace. In the same way a football coach develops the plays and coaches each player to perform at optimal levels, you need a coach to help you learn how to navigate the organization. My first experience with someone coaching me outside of my company was when I started to give presentations as a part of my interview process in higher education. Many times, the final round of interviews

was a 30- to 45-minute presentation to the team I would potentially work with on a best practice, idea, or solution to a current problem within the department. I've always loved presenting and public speaking, but doing this to seal the deal on a job was a completely different ball game. As my career grew, the stakes only got higher with each presentation. The expectations rose, and the level of stakeholders in the room also elevated. During this time, I leaned on the coaches in my career to provide specific feedback and help improve my presentations' content and caliber. It was not enough to have a mentor. I needed someone to coach me on how to assemble the presentation, provide feedback when I rehearsed it, and ensure I was prepared to answer questions from various stakeholder perspectives. Coaches can also be mentors for some professionals, but not every mentor can be a coach.

3. *Mentors*: Mentors are the category of relationship that most people are familiar with and actively seek. The main difference between a mentor relationship and other key relationship types is that a mentor must have been in your shoes at some point in his or her career. Mentors can guide you through many situations based on first-hand experiences. In my experience, many professionals have former managers who remain mentors throughout their careers. Some have a standing meeting, while others check in from time to time. Some professionals participate in formalized mentorship programs through their college, company, or professional organization, whereas others find mentors on their own. An important fact to note is that you do not have to ask someone to be your mentor. *Many professionals feel like they need to have a formalized conversation about securing a mentor, but really, mentorship is about the caliber of the relationship and the content of the conversations that happen.* If you have regular meetings with a professional who can help you navigate day-to-day problems in your career, you have a mentor, even if that's not what you call him or her.

4. *Sponsors*: Over the past few years, I've been excited to see the sponsorship conversation become more prevalent. When speaking about workplace relationships, people have usually advised to network and find a mentor. Now, we also talk about the other types of needed relationships, and sponsors have come to the forefront of that conversation. *Sponsors are people who can take you from where you are right now to the next step in your career strategy. They have the power to advocate for you in rooms that you have not been invited to, and they influence key stakeholders who can significantly impact your career.* Generally, sponsors are often senior professionals in the office who have the impact, influence, and power to make decisions. This may be your manager's manager or even higher. It would also be common for you not to interact with these leaders frequently, but you know they are important, and every minute counts when you get a moment on their calendar. For some professionals, sponsors can also be mentors, but not every mentor has the influence to be a sponsor.

Last but not least, I'd like to reinforce that you do not need to have direct contact with coaches and mentors. Essentially, they can be role models. It's always important to have relationships with professionals who know and interact with you, but for coaches and mentors, you can also be supported through the advice, tips, and best practices these professionals virtually share with you. In those cases, I consider those professionals as "role models." A role model in my career is Oprah Winfrey. I've followed her career, read her magazine, watched episodes of her show, and listened to her podcasts. I've taken copious notes on the stories and actionable steps she shares, and I've implemented them in my career and life. Although I haven't had the pleasure (yet) of meeting Oprah, I can 100% say she has influenced my life.

Now that you understand the different types of relationships, I invite you to list the relationships you have in each category. Ideally, having two to three professionals in each category is a great start. As a reminder, you should arrange your relationships under these four categories:

1. Peers
2. Coaches
3. Mentors
4. Sponsors

If you have an area that does not have existing relationships, it's time to do some research to identify professionals to reach out to or to consume readily available books, podcasts, or resources that you can learn from. A hidden network of people to connect with may be your high school or college alumni network. When you were applying to college, you can probably recall many admissions officers touting their school's "strong alumni network." And for good reason: Alumni can be incredibly influential not only when you're an undergraduate, but after graduation. This is another network of professionals whom you already have a common connection with.

If you're reading this book and are a current student or recent graduate, connecting with alumni can seem intimidating. Remember: the No. 1 way to leverage your school's network is to be part of it. Many graduates forget to update their contact information after moving off campus and entering the workforce. Make sure to send your new email and mailing address to your university's alumni office. If you're not on the list for monthly newsletters, mailings for homecoming, or any other notifications, you'll miss out on key opportunities to get involved. Even if you've graduated more than 10 years ago, it's still great to keep in touch.

Often after graduation, many professionals end up receiving calls or mail about making financial donations, but no matter how long ago you've graduated, that may not be feasible. While you may not be able to write a check, look for unique ways to donate your time. Many alumni stay connected through mentoring, volunteering at campus events, or hosting current students for workplace site visits.

If you're still unsure of how to connect with alumni or your college doesn't have a directory, I always recommend using LinkedIn to track down alumni who are at specific companies, geographic locations, or industries. Sometimes just going to the same college is the only common ground you need to strike up a conversation.

As a reminder, when reaching out to fellow alumni, be sure to take an interest in them personally and professionally. Don't just ask them if they can hire you or connect you with someone who can hire you. You'll gain far more career advice – and maybe even a lifelong mentor – when a true relationship is cultivated.

As you think about the gaps in your relationships, part of your career strategy will be to ensure these relationships stay at the front of your mind. It's not enough to make a connection. You must conduct regular upkeep to create a long-lasting relationship.

Part Three

Establish a personal and professional brand that aligns with where you want to go.

Chapter 7

Building Your Career Strategy

Career Affirmation: I am building a successful career strategy to support my goals.

Seasons do not end when you're finished with traditional schooling. The average professional with a collegiate degree has spent 16 to 20 years in some form of traditional schooling, which means adhering to the cycle of fall, winter break, spring, and summer break – rinse and repeat, year after year – a pattern we've learned to accept. Before we enter the workforce, we receive more "insider information" through the syllabus that each professor provides at the beginning of the semester. The syllabus shares exactly what is needed to pass the class successfully. If you follow the syllabus, plan to study, and submit your assignments on time, you should earn a good grade. If you ignore the syllabus and allow it to lay crumpled at the bottom of your bag with leftover chip crumbs and gum wrappers, the entire semester will feel like an awful surprise, and it will be extremely hard to do well. As that last year of college comes faster than you would have ever imagined, intense conversations arise about "getting the job." The consulting, finance, and big-tech students get offer letters before Thanksgiving (or earlier) due to how the recruiting season works at big banks, technology, and consulting firms. The remainder of the student population does its best to secure placement before graduation in May.

Meanwhile, your parents have been happily and excitedly talking about you "leaving the nest," which adds to the pressure. Then, after several rounds of interviews, you enter the workforce without a syllabus, generally without mentorship, and hope that everything works itself out through hard work and a kind manager who can show you the ropes if you're lucky. After all, the hardest part is getting the job, right?

In most cases, this is all wrong.

The hardest part of the process isn't finding a job that does more than pay well. The hardest part is finding a job that allows you to build a career. I've found that it's extremely helpful to have "insider information." *Insider information helps us determine the norms or seasons in your industry or company.* When referencing insider information, I don't just mean the information needed to get an interview or job offer. I'm referring to the information that allows you to do the following:

- Navigate office politics with ease
- Identify key stakeholders you need to avoid interactions with or get to know
- Move into more senior-level roles strategically

Insider information is the missing information that many professionals underestimate when building their careers. As a career coach, I have many career-related conversations with friends and family. Whether that conversation takes place while waiting in line for food at the family BBQ or over wine with girlfriends, I lend an objective ear to learn more about how professionals feel they should navigate the world of work. One of my "soapbox" conversations when I can't help but give "straight talk, no chaser" advice, is when someone believes he or she doesn't need relationships to build a thriving career strategy. The first argument normally goes something like this:

> *Kimberly, I do not need to like everyone at my job. I'm there to do my job and go home. I'm not trying to make friends, and I'm definitely not going to sit at happy hour to listen to Jack's bad dad jokes when I could be home with my friends and family.*

Sound familiar?

I know Jack's dad jokes are terrible. Trust me, I've heard them myself, but I always stress that building relationships has absolutely nothing to do with the quality of those jokes. Building relationships has to do with learning more about the people who make up the organization. Building relationships has to do with understanding the games that are being played at your organization and making sure "the coach," aka your manager or company leadership, knows you're ready to be a starting player. *A vital piece of a thriving career strategy has to do with understanding your work and where it fits within the organization's larger picture.* That's what relationships can do for you, and that's why they must be a part of your career strategy.

My mom used to tell my dad "No man is an island" because he wasn't one to socialize with neighbors. Once you were in with my dad, you became family, but it wasn't until the relationship crossed that threshold that my dad even cared.

Growing up, we had a huge garden in our backyard. Dad would plant everything, including lettuce, corn, eggplant, potatoes, watermelon, beans, peas, fruit trees, and tons of crops I rarely ate if they were green. There was almost always a surplus, but Dad would wash and freeze them instead of sharing with the neighbors. Mom always asked him to share, but he wasn't having that. He froze his produce so we would have fresh, homegrown vegetables in the winter. As for the fruit, he made all types of jams for his homemade bread. By the fall, I remember the freezer being overloaded with vegetables, and Dad turned a closet into a canning room for all the preserves and jams he made in our basement. A few neighbors and my friends' parents began to creep their way into my dad's heart over the years. He would bundle up a care package of fruits, vegetables, and jams for them when they would come over in the summer and fall months. He took pride in sharing what he harvested from our family garden. My neighbors and friends' parents' relationships were built over 18 years, from the day I was adopted until the day I left for college. He built similar relationships with my younger sister's friends' parents too, but as I think about the length of time it took my dad to build those friendships in our neighborhood, I realize we have nowhere near that amount of time to cultivate relationships in the workforce. With many professionals changing jobs every two to five years, you don't have the luxury of waiting.

While you have your head down, working until the late evening on projects you believe will make or break your career, there are other professionals who are also working hard on their projects but simultaneously prioritizing relationships and ensuring that lunch and early-morning coffee runs are spent getting to know someone in the office. In a virtual environment, they prioritize virtual coffee chats and happy hours to ensure they build new relationships and keep up with old ones. By the time this book is in your hands in Spring 2021, many workplaces will still have nonessential employees working virtually due to COVID-19; a virtual environment is not a reason to deprioritize building relationships.

You also can't rely on your manager, human resources department, or mentor to build a career strategy for you. You must go after the information you need to support the career you would like to build for yourself. In Chapter 4, I talked about identifying your short- and long-term goals, and in Chapter 6, relationship building was covered. Now, it's time to put it all together to assemble your strategy.

When we think about career strategies, we often expect the strategy to be handed to us by senior leadership, human resources, a direct manager, or a mentor building it out on our behalf. Still, I want to empower you to understand the importance of putting together your strategy. This strategy will focus on your goals and align with your career opportunities, not only for your career at your current company but for your overall career. Additionally, relationships are a key part of your career strategy to help you navigate new situations and easily move into your next opportunities. If you do not believe in the power of relationship building in your career, I hope digging into the concept of insider information will help you understand that this career concept is nonnegotiable for you.

I affectionately call my email newsletter "insider notes" because it's my way of sharing career-related stories, insight, experiences, and tips with my subscribers. In your everyday life, insider information is the same thing. Essentially, insider information is the 15-minute coffee chat when you learn more about a stakeholder and his or her preferences for receiving information for a new business proposals or those quick after-hour drinks when you get some helpful feedback to learn a better way to approach your role. *As you build relationships with peers, coaches, mentors, and sponsors, the insider information you receive will make or break your ability to take advantage of various opportunities.* For example, whenever I learned about a new career opportunity, the first thing I would do was go through my network to determine if I knew anyone working with or for the company to conduct an informational interview. As a professional in the workforce, you know there's a big difference between the beautiful job descriptions and testimonials on the company website versus the actual experience working at a company, especially as a woman or person of color. Once I locate a contact or request an introduction from someone we have in common, I prepare key questions to inform my next steps. Typically, I ask questions like these:

- *Would you share your current experience in the company?*
- *Do you feel your experience has been consistent since day one?*
- *What are the policies for upward movement at your company?*
- *Would you share more about your experiences with senior leadership?*
- *Do you feel like you have opportunities to grow at this company?*
- *Do you feel like there's a glass ceiling for women and people of color? If yes, why?*

If the person works in the same team or department that I'm seeking to work in, I also ask the following:

- *Would you tell me more about the leadership style of the manager?*
- *What are the biggest challenges your team faces?*
- *Who are the key stakeholders and external teams your team works with?*
- *Does your manager have any red flags he or she looks for in candidates? If so, would you identify them?*
- *What do you believe the first 90 days in this role will look like?*

When you rely on your company to build your career strategy, you allow it to have a singular focus for your career. Your company spends thousands upon thousands of dollars recruiting and onboarding its talent. So, of course, it likes to ensure it keeps it, which means its priority will be to keep you in your role or a promotional role within that same department or company at-large. Moreover, companies frequently focus exclusively on developing their high-potential talent. High potential can have several meanings, depending on the company, but what I've seen, especially for women and people of color, is that although they do phenomenal work, they may not have the talent designation of "high potential." High potential is short for:

- Ready for a promotional opportunity
- Ready for a new, lateral opportunity
- Ready to begin managing people
- Ready for a stretch assignment
- Needs more development but is very promising, and efforts need to be made to retain the talent, so the employee does not pursue external opportunities

After more than 11 years of career development experience in higher education, talent acquisition, and coaching hundreds of clients, I have seen that many companies do not have strict guidelines on the definition of high potential. *Without high-potential definitions to remove bias and allow managers to make an objective assessment of their talent, that talent is being evaluated at the mercy of the managers.*

I've had some great managers and some terrible managers in my career, and one of the best pieces of advice I received was from one of my mentors, a senior executive at a Fortune 100 Company. *She advised that not all feedback is about me.* When she shared this during a conversation, my mind was blown. I had an experience in my office that I wanted to review with her, and she changed the way I thought about performance appraisals and feedback in the workplace. Managers are responsible for providing feedback and insights about their teams that can make or break a team member's career. However, a biased opinion can paint a picture of a team member that does not align with that member's skill set, performance, and career objectives.

In that same conversation, my mentor also spoke candidly about what it means to be a Black woman in corporate America. Moreover, she spoke to my specific experience as an accomplished professional who runs a company outside of my traditional day job. I love to explain my journey to entrepreneurship by saying that I've been playing around on the Internet since 2011. There have been several iterations of Manifest Yourself before the blog really turned into a company around 2013. However, the consistent topic has always been personal development. In 2013, I finally opted to include the professional development piece since my love for career and leadership development provided me with experiences outside of my 9-to-5 role in higher education. Over the more recent years, I've moved from coaching women and people of color individually to providing organizations with tailor-made solutions to hire, develop, engage, and retain women and people of color. My niche is making sure professionals know how to navigate the workplace, negotiate their salaries, and position themselves as leaders. Whether I'm working with one person, an employee resource group, or an entire organization, I believe professionals need to possess these core skills.

As my company grew, I was no longer able to hide my "side hustle" because of my online presence and that ruffled some feathers. Regardless of my performance in the office, other leaders projected their opinions into conversations about my performance. While I never thought that my external experiences would become a breeding ground for biased feedback about my work performance, my mentor reiterated that many leaders in the organization may feel threatened. Early on in my career, I was used to having conversations about my social media use "in the office," explaining that I had a social media intern or assistant who preloaded content into my scheduling software and responded to comments while I was at work so I wasn't using company time even if it appeared that way. But as Manifest Yourself grew, the conversations became much more serious – sometimes leading to conversations with company legal and public affairs departments, and my manager.

I've always prided myself in never cobranding myself using my 9-to-5 company name in any of my business materials, but that was no longer enough.

For example, if I did not perform well on a project, my feedback would be regarding my outside business instead of specific feedback about improving the deliverables. Basically, managers would suggest that if I spent more time focused on my role in my day job, then maybe the project would have been much better. In truth, though, I may have had a lack of understanding about the project, and regardless of whether I spent my evenings working to improve the project or on a new sales funnel for my business, it would have never been any better because I did not have the insight needed to take the project to the next level. When I think back on my career, I can think of several circumstances when a similar conversation took place, but again, I don't know if the feedback was for me. All I could do was continue to do great work and seek out objective feedback to apply when needed.

I've always taken pride in maintaining a thriving 9-to-5 career and a growing business, but I can't lie and say that this has been easy. Moreover, when it comes to building your own career strategy, both having a side hustle and climbing the proverbial ladder in your industry need to be considered if they are both equally important to you. So, I ask you – do you want your career strategy to be based on the insights of a manager who may or may not have his or her own biases impacting your high-potential-talent designation, or do you want to create a strategy built for you by you, to ensure an unbiased look at the opportunities available to you throughout the trajectory of your career?

Your Next Move

It's time to finally start building your career strategy. Up to this point in the book, we've focused on various elements of your strategy, but now we will bring out your pen and paper to assemble a document you will continue to iterate through the end of this book or you can go to nextmovebestmovebook.com to download an editable copy of the template I share with you in Chapter 13. A career strategy is comprised of four key elements:

1. **Your self-assessment to identify your strengths and weaknesses:** In Chapter 2, we dug into your past experiences to learn about the skills you've acquired throughout your career. Through the "Your Next Move" section, you were able to get clarity on the skills you would like to use moving forward and the skills you would like to limit the use of in your next career move. In Chapter 5, we talked about the gap between where you are and where you would like to go. The gaps in your knowledge, experiences, and skills are just as important as your skills. As a manager who thoroughly enjoys managing people, when a candidate cannot talk about his or her weaknesses or gaps in experiences, I can quickly see that he or she is not self-aware. I always joke to myself that I'll be able to determine people's weaknesses within the first 90 days of working with them, and if they were able to articulate that in the interview, I would have been able to build a plan for how to get them up to speed more efficiently. *Your weaknesses and knowledge gaps won't always prevent you from getting the job.* If it's truly an experiential gap, you may need to prepare yourself appropriately by attacking that, and create a plan for it as part of your career strategy. Professionals should not strive to be in roles where they are in over their head at work because they were ill-prepared but did not want to share that in an interview. Better yet, if you knew you were ill-prepared, it's best to apply to jobs that align with your core values and strengths to ensure your success and continue to position yourself as a leader while developing the skills needed for the promotional role that may have been a bit too large of a stretch at that time. There's a huge difference between being challenged in a role, which is healthy in any career transition, and being in over your head, where

you can't seem to bridge the gap between where you are now and where you are expected to perform in the new role. Before moving to the next step, make sure you have a list of your strengths, weaknesses, and gaps between your current role and your next logical role.

2. **Your professional brand (and learning how to showcase it):** Once you know more about your strengths, weaknesses, and gaps, it's time to take a deeper look into your personal and professional brand. As with the last process, we will take a deeper look into this in Chapter 8 to determine if your brand reflects your goals.

3. **Elevating your authority:** Knowing that you have a great personal and professional brand that aligns with your career goals is not enough. You must elevate your authority within your industry. We will cover how to do this in Chapter 9.

4. **Creating clear, short- and long-term objectives:** This is what we covered in Chapter 4. To map out your initial career strategy, we must know where you would like to go. Although your five-year goal will most likely be a moving target, we need a beginning and end to start the process.

Now that you have the four key steps, it's time to put them together! Please skip to the end of Chapter 13, "Put It All Together," to begin filling out the template to start building your career strategy or go to nextmovebestmovebook.com to download an editable copy of the template. Again, this is not something that will be fully completed until the end of the book, but it's important to start putting your pen to paper right now to incorporate what has been discussed thus far.

Please note that the chart will go from planning six months at a time to jumping to two years and then five years. This is because you may end up changing and reevaluating your plan based on your progress within the next 18 months.

This is a purposeful, intentional document. I strongly encourage you to revisit and edit as you see fit, so if it's been smooth sailing for the first 18 months, feel free to continue to build out your strategy in six-month increments. *Do not be afraid to "go for the stretch" and challenge yourself with your career strategy if you have a specific career goal in mind.* If you've edited your plan significantly, start at your career's updated current state and build things out in six-month increments. If you are unsure of the tasks you need to complete, this would be a great time to reach out to your coaches and mentors to help you fill out the tasks you need to accomplish. Generally, this is where my clients focus on the following:

- Mastering a system or software
- Mastering a skill
- Completing a degree or certification program
- Developing relationships with a stakeholder
- Identifying and cultivating relationships with coaches, mentors, or sponsors
- Identifying and cultivating relationships in professional organizations

The possibilities are endless! However, be specific. You will not be able to measure your success or determine if you've reached a milestone if you don't get specific.

Chapter 8

Your Personal and Professional "Experience" – A Deeper Look into Personal and Professional Branding

Career Affirmation: I have a strong personal and professional brand that attracts relationships and organizations that support my career.

What experience do you provide those who interact with you?

That is the first question I ask any client who works with me to build his or her personal and professional brand. When discussing this topic, people often think more about self-promotion versus personal and professional branding. My clients are often solely focused on how to best promote whatever it is they need when interacting with new contacts. They ask themselves questions like:

- *How can I show my value when I don't have a lot of experience?*
- *How do I ask for mentorship or sponsorship?*
- *How do I explain the work that I do?*

Instead of focusing on those questions, I encourage them to focus on creating an experience that allows any professional to understand his or her personal and professional brand from multiple viewpoints. *When you remove the need to "sell" or "promote" yourself, relationship building can feel much less stressful.*

In one of the early interviews in my career, I recall an interviewer who truly rattled my confidence. The interview was going fine until one person asked, "What are your strengths and weaknesses?" I had prepared for the interview and was comfortable providing the standard response of three strengths and three weaknesses. For my strengths, I articulated how I had cultivated those strengths in past roles. Then, I provided brief examples. For the weaknesses, I shared the actionable ways I was working to improve them. This was how I always articulated the answer to this question, and my answer had worked in several interviews, leading me to land the respective job.

This time, however, one of the interviewers on the panel looked at me and said, "Are those the only things you're good at?"

I was beside myself when I heard the interviewer's response. I recall rattling off a few other strengths that I felt were strong, but I was so caught off guard that I knew my nerves were showing, and I could not shake my embarrassment. Many young professionals, when they make one mistake in an interview, are so focused on their bad response that they continue to make more mistakes and feel like they're tumbling down a hill for the remainder of the interview. That was me – uncontrollably tumbling down a massive hill, tripping over my own feet and not able to stand upright for the rest of the interview. After the interview, I cried inside my car because I was so set on nailing the interview, but I knew I was thrown off by the interviewer's follow-up question. Now, I realize I had given surface-level responses to these questions.

My mistake at the time was that I listed commonplace strengths like being a hard worker or having a bachelor's degree in business management that was not only a requirement but had prepared me for the role. Yes, you are a hard worker, but so are the other candidates for the job. Instead of giving generic, safe answers, your personal and professional brand needs to connect to the experience you create when anyone interacts with you. Better yet, your brand is the reason someone hires you for the role. *Personal branding is the manifestation of your skill set and the impact it has on the workplace.* Even if you sell the same product or interview for the same role as someone else, you must think about your unique skill set and impact. So, again, what is the experience you provide to anyone who interacts with you?

Also, please take note that I use personal and professional brand together and interchangeably because you are who you are, whether you are in the office, at home, or among friends. You may find yourself "code-switching" in some scenarios, but there will always be a few elements of yourself that you may not be able to bring into the office, and that's natural. Some professionals may disagree, but I cannot see myself treating my co-workers at happy hour in the same manner I treat my best girlfriends at happy hour. Even when some work environments are casual, there is always an element of seriousness because your actions in the workplace, even with your "work wife," "work husband," or office best friend, can impact your career trajectory.

When thinking about your professional brand's key elements, I like to break it down to your internal and external sides. Regarding your internal side, that is more about your character and actions. Those are the elements of your brand that are innate to who you are. No matter what environment you are in, personal or professional, these elements stay consistent. On the external side are your experiences and skills. These are the external experiences you gain throughout your career and education to utilize in any role. As you continue to gain experiences and skills, you will continue to grow the external side of your brand. When we put it together, I always say that your internal work plus your external qualifications come together to build an excellent personal and professional brand.

If we back up a little more, you will discover that your character is comprised of qualities distinctive to your individuality or core values, which we covered in Chapter 3. When you think about yourself, inside and outside of work, what are your core values? Values may include being emotionally open and self-confident and having a lot of discipline or generosity. Those qualities are innate and really do not change, whether you are in the workplace or at home.

When we look at our actions, we learn that actions involve processes of doing something. When you try to achieve a goal, what actions do you take? When you get up to go to work, what are typical actions that manifest no matter what you do? These are actions such as showing up on time and providing honest feedback to others.

While I was in high school, I had a band teacher with a signature phrase he repeated before all concerts and events – "Early is on time, and on time is late." He believed in this phrase so much that he had no problem leaving you behind if you were late. If you showed up late when the bus was leaving the school for a trip, you would be greeted by an empty high school parking lot. This always reinforced his point that lateness had consequences. So, since hearing my teacher's signature phrase, no matter where I am as a professional, wife, sister, daughter, and friend, I believe that early is on time, and on time is late. That's a consistent action I always take no matter where I am that also drives the standard of work I bring to any team I'm on.

Another common action for me is the desire to pursue developmental opportunities. I'm always the first to raise my hand to attend a professional development webinar, event, or training. I love to learn ways to improve my work and scale my own leadership capabilities. Are you big on investing in yourself and others? Given that you are reading this book, I'm sure you believe in personal and professional development, so investing in yourself is very important. You are most likely to seek other developmental opportunities in your personal and work life to ensure you are informed and equipped to handle whatever comes your way.

As we move to the external side, we see that this is your practical experience, inside and outside the workplace. This is the career you have built, the past jobs you've had, and the side-hustle you are building. Your external side could also be volunteer work, experiences in a professional organization, extracurricular activities, internships, training programs, coursework, and degree programs, the things you have done throughout your career and educational background that contribute to your identity.

On the other side of the external piece is skills. When talking about personal and professional branding, skills are more about your abilities, and, as you know, your experiences are vastly different from your abilities. For example, throughout middle school and high school, I took advanced-level math classes. My parents were both educators and believed that math was an important subject, so I grew up going to a learning center to advance my math skills. Just because I took advanced math classes does not mean I'm good at math. I've struggled with math my entire life, whether it was a complex math problem to pass an assessment for a new job or understanding equations in a spreadsheet. Math is not something I would list as a skill, even though I have a lot of experience with math. However, I have always been a writer – keeping journals, off and on since I was a teenager, writing songs, and now writing a book!

If you are unsure of what you consider your skills, I challenge you to think about the things your co-workers look to you for help with. What is that thing you do that your manager relies on you to complete? What are the tasks you breeze through while you see other peers struggling? Experiences and skills make up the external side of your personal and professional brand.

As we dig into your personal and professional brand, the next question I want you to ask yourself is, "Is my personal and professional brand what I would like for it to be?" When I go back and think about my personal and professional brand, I think about every career transition I've ever made. When I started my career in financial services, as I shared earlier, I quickly found out that it was not the career for me because I didn't enjoy sales, so I moved into higher education. After spending nearly 10 years in higher education, I was interested in moving into corporate America. Although my personal and professional brand was closely tied to the work, experiences, and skills I built in higher education, I had to shift a bit to ensure my brand was better aligned to the role I wanted in corporate America. *If your brand is not aligned with the next move you would like to make, you've got some work to do. Your brand can change as you grow and evolve as a professional in the workforce.*

One of the top pieces of information I share about personal branding is that personal and professional branding can open a closed door. *Exceptions can always be made for greatness because no one wants to hire someone mediocre.* In all my years of hiring, I've never looked to hire the person who was second best or could almost do the job. I always want to hire the best. Working in talent acquisition, I frequently have conversations about the interview process and how candidates perform. Most recruiters' pet peeve is candidates who come in with the "Please, baby, baby, please" mentality. This mentality is when candidates come into interviews hoping for a chance to get to the next level versus aligning themselves with the level they would like to operate in or the role they would like to obtain. During the interview process, these candidates concentrate on getting the opportunity because they are ready to rise to the occasion, rather than showcasing their skill set and professional brand in a way that best aligns with the role and company.

As you think about your brand, it's important to understand where you are, where you would like to be, and the gap between the two. As you read this, if you are still unclear on your gap, I want you to think about how you're showing up at work, after work, with friends and family, with colleagues, at the gym, with your partner or spouse, when you have big goals, when you want to get a promotion, when you are angry, when you are unmotivated, and when you are overwhelmed. *How you show up is a big part of your personal and professional brand because it is part of the experience that other people have when interacting with you.* When you put this information together, you start to get clear on your personal and professional brand and how your brand manifests in the workplace. When you are clear on your personal and professional brand, it's very easy to start putting together a mission and vision for yourself or update your LinkedIn profile summary. *You must know and understand yourself before asking other people to understand who you are in the workplace.*

To fast-forward a bit, when we talk about salary negotiation, many people think that it's really about that final conversation when the recruiter or hiring manager offers you the role and shares the total compensation. The recruiter/hiring manager is super excited and begins the conversation like this: "Hey, Kimberly! I'm so excited to offer you this position. We are delighted to give you a salary offer of $120,000 per year. What do you say? I'd love to have you on my team." Many professionals think that is where salary negotiation begins. However, salary negotiation begins the moment you interact with the company through your personal and professional brand.

If you are being head-hunted for a role or are interested in a company and have informational interviews or research people online, your brand will begin to speak before you do. Recruiters or hiring leaders may look up your LinkedIn profile or past conference presentations and figure out what other organizations you are involved with before they reach out to you. Having a personal and professional brand that is clear, online and offline, is really important.

Regarding offline personal and professional branding, this is when someone will reach out to a mentor or contact of yours to ask about their experience working with you and if they believe you are a good fit for the role. If your personal and professional brand is unclear, your mentor or contact will not be able to advocate for you. Your brand needs to speak for itself and be clear for anyone who has a stake in your career to share more about your character, actions, skills, and experiences. Like a formal letter of reference, you never want a lukewarm response when anyone asks about who you are as a professional. *Again, personal and professional branding sets the stage for the type of salary you can negotiate. I always reinforce that your goal is to get a great offer instead of fighting tooth and nail for the company to raise the initial offer.* You want the company to be so excited to bring you in that you receive an already great offer. If you do your research and learn that you can negotiate a bit more, go ahead and do so. All this starts by having a clear personal and professional brand.

Your Next Move

The first step I want you to take is assessing where you are and where you would like to be in each step of your career strategy document. Similar to how we assessed your current career destination in Chapter 3 before we began to outline steps in your career strategy document, we need to get clear on the experience you are currently providing before we understand the experience you would like to provide.

Think about how people experience you and your work in the workplace. This may be a good time to reference your last performance appraisal or review from your manager when they provided you with direct feedback on your performance over the past year or six months. Take note of the feedback provided during this time. If you do not have a formal performance appraisal process, I suggest reaching out to your manager, department heads, colleagues, or peers to ask them for some feedback on your performance. I encourage you to ask at least three to five professionals the following questions:

1. What has your experience been like working with me?
2. What should I do more of in my role?
3. What should I do less of in my role?
4. If someone were to reach out for feedback on your experience working with me, what are three adjectives you would use to describe me and my work?

If you are speaking with your direct manager, do not forget to ask:

What would you need to see from me to be eligible for a promotion in the future?

The key in asking this last question is being quiet after you ask it. You want to hear what your manager has to say so you can incorporate this into your career plan. Even if he or she shares some tasks that you know you're already doing, this may give you a hint that you may need to raise the level of visibility of those skills or tasks to ensure your manager sees and acknowledges your work.

Next, I want you to think about where you would like to be in your career within the next one to two years. Is it another role? Is it in another company? Wherever it is, think about the person whom the company is looking to hire for that role. Based on the earlier conversations you had with professionals in similar roles, how does that experience differ from yours? This may require research, but it's well worth it to ensure that you align your professional experiences to reflect where you would like to be in the future. Ask yourself the following questions:

• *When I compare my experiences to professionals in my field in my dream roles, what differences do I see in their character, actions, skills, and experience?*

- *When reviewing the differences, is there anything I would like to add to my career strategy plan?*

Before we fall into a deep, dark hole of comparison, I want to reiterate that you are using like-minded professionals' experiences as a guide to learn more about your field of interest. This is not intended for you to beat yourself up about the differences or not showcase your special sauce. Every professional has his or her own special sauce because we are all individuals! Instead, this information should help you make the most informed decisions. There is no reason to wing it when someone out there can help you navigate the journey to achieve your goals.

If you are still unclear, this may also be the perfect time to have an informational conversation with recruiters in your organization to understand the profile of an individual that they look for when hiring for the next role you are seeking. In many organizations, recruiters are responsible for identifying, screening, and conducting the first round of interviews for candidates before passing them along to the hiring manager. They have some of the best insight on candidates selected to interview with the hiring manager and ultimately selected to receive an offer letter. Great recruiters will highlight key skills and experiences that you should leverage in the interview process or that you may need to cultivate before applying for lateral or promotional opportunities.

The most frequent example I share about leveraging another professional's experience or attributes is from my entrepreneurial journey. As an entrepreneur, I had no idea what I was doing in the beginning. I was confused and figuring it out along the way until I learned about business coaches. In most cases, business coaches have mastered a specific skill and have built a framework or process that they teach to help others do the same. At first, I was fine with stumbling and figuring it out until I realized I could invest in a coach to teach me the processes I was missing. It's not that I was modeling my business exactly after the coach's business, but I could apply their frameworks to my business and make it my own. The same thing applies to your professional career. One of the biggest mistakes professionals make is waiting for the opportunity to show up, but as discussed earlier, it's important to show up now. Do not wait until the job is on the line, and you are moments away from the interview. Expecting yourself to rise to the occasion without preparation and insider information to step into this new version of yourself is unrealistic. You want to make sure you are clear on your personal and professional brand and strengths and weaknesses to ensure that you are ready whenever the opportunity comes.

Part Four

Put your plan into action and advocate for yourself in the workplace.

Chapter 9

How to Bring It All Together and Put It Out in the World

Career Affirmation: My personal mission and vision will positively impact the lives of others.

I'm sure you've read a lot about various career tactics and research opportunities to determine the next steps in your career strategy to ensure your next move is your best move, but now it's time to focus on putting all these things together to teach you how to deliver your best to the world. The first time I became clear about having a brand in the workplace was the first time I presented at a conference. I didn't know anything about professional development conferences until I got into career services in my first role as a career development counselor.

In this role, I worked on an assessment project with my manager to think about whether we could measure student learning in career development classes. Our university had a class that walked our students through best practices and prepared them to search for internship opportunities. The class was a pass/fail, four-week experience that was always taught in person. Since the class was pass/fail, many students did not prioritize attendance or feel committed to completing homework assignments. Knowing this, we wanted to test teaching the class in an online environment within the same timeframe but self-paced so students could complete the assignments when most convenient. This was a huge shift in learning for our career services team.

Fast-forward to 2020, when much of the professional workforce and college campuses shifted to remote work and learning to reduce the spread of COVID-19; moving to remote learning sounds like it wouldn't be a major issue, but during my time in this role as a career development counselor, this was something that wasn't done frequently. The big question at the time was whether students could truly learn career development best practices online.

I worked on a project teaching two versions of the class: one in person and one online. We tested student learning through quizzes and interactive exercises to compare quiz scores of students who participated in online classes versus students in the in-person classes with a career development counselor. This study led to my first opportunity to present the findings at a career development conference. It was an unspoken rule that counselors generally did not attend conferences unless they were presenting or serving as a board member. However, to serve as a board member, I needed to attend a conference to know more about the organization and its members to ensure it was a community I wanted to join. So, I asked my supervisor if I would be able to apply to present at a conference for the New York State Cooperative and Experiential Education Association.

Before that time, I really believed that if you did good work and put your head down, you would take your career to the next level. As long as your manager knew the work that you were doing and your team appreciated you, that was really all you needed. Through this conference, I learned that presenting outside of the office and sharing the work I did in my role were great ways to position myself and allow other professionals to experience my personal and professional brand.

Essentially, this is the opposite of the "making moves in silence" mindset. Similar to how Beyoncé dropped her fifth studio album without any promotion, this mindset is about keeping your head down, doing good work, and hoping that when you "drop" something impactful others will notice. However, to continue with the Beyoncé example, she had four previous solo albums and her career with Destiny's Child to prepare her audience for a secret album. She knew the excitement would work in her favor for her fan base. Have you prepared your professional audience so that you when you "make a move in silence" you'll still be able to reap the rewards?

I always joke that many hardworking professionals, especially in minority communities, put their head down, work, and hope they will be granted the opportunity to move into another role. Still, as many of us now know, that is not the case. You must "play the game," and the game is so much more than office politics. *Amplifying and sharing your work and personal and professional brand are large parts of this*. When I presented at the conference with my colleague, Amber, this changed my career trajectory.

After presenting at the conference, dozens of professionals came up to us and asked questions about our experiences of teaching online and offline. They wanted more information and insight from our quizzes and the curriculum we had built on for online and in-person classes and what they could do to implement the best practices we shared at their university. I was mind blown that people would want to talk to me, an entry-level career advisor, to learn best practices to implement at their institutions. This was less about the recognition of a job well done but more of a realization that my work could impact career counselors outside of my university.

Our presentation had wonderful reviews from conference attendees, so much so that attendees continued to talk about our work the next morning over breakfast. It was a smaller-scale conference with fewer than 150 professionals, so the community was tight-knit, and the board was able to get real-time feedback from attendees. Amber and I were sitting at a table eating breakfast, and many of the board members came and asked us a few questions about our career goals and interest in the industry, ultimately asking us to join the board. It happened so fast that I barely remember agreeing to join the board! At that time, I had no idea what being on a board would be like, but I knew if it would connect me with more like-minded professionals and continue to position myself as a leader, it would be good for me.

After speaking at that conference and joining the board, I was able to really start the process of elevating my career to the next level. To this day, I am appreciative of the New York State Cooperative and Experiential Education Association for how I was able to advance in career services from a small-scale conference to working at Ivy League institutions. This experience taught me that you must expand your brand outside of your job. *It's not okay to keep your head down and work every day without connecting with professionals in your industry.* Through those relationships, I learned about other organizations and leadership opportunities. I started in that organization as a director of publicity and was responsible for putting together all the email marketing, social media, and publicity management. It was extremely easy work at the time, but little did

I know, the board was preparing me for the vice president role, the most work-intensive role within the organization. The vice president of this organization was responsible for planning the annual conference.

At the next conference, the year after my first presentation and board appointment, I celebrated in the current vice president's hotel suite. Attending a conference as an attendee and board member was a new experience for me. I was more invested in the organization's success and ensuring that I met and spoke with attendees from all over New York. The conversations I had were less about networking and more about building true relationships. I had participated in monthly calls with the board to prepare for the conference, so after a year of connecting, they were more like friends than fellow board members. I was also aware of the professionals who attended the conference, the speakers selected to present workshops, and the staff that was instrumental in ensuring the conference's logistics. This conference was more like a reunion.

As we celebrated the conference's success in the vice president's suite that evening, the board joked about how I should be the next vice president conference chair. Somewhere between good laughs, thinking about what next year could look like, and a few glasses of wine, it was decided that I would run for vice president and the conference would be in Westchester, New York, to accommodate the members located in the Greater New York City area and upstate New York. The following morning, at breakfast, I was handed a large bin of the organization's governance documents and was officially running for the vice president role – unopposed.

If you've ever planned an annual conference for an organization or attended a conference, you may have an idea of this project's magnitude. Planning an annual conference was the largest task I had handled in my career up to that point, and this was in addition to my full-time job. This stretched me beyond any capacity I thought was possible but also gave me an opportunity to allow my personal and professional brand to shine and expand through the relationships built during that time. The following year, I was beaming with pride throughout the conference. I saw my work pay off in the face of every attendee and the board members who helped me plan for the event and validated that all of my work paid off for the greater good of the NYSCEEA community.

After the annual conference, I had the pleasure of hosting the board in my own suite with wine and snacks. In the same fashion that I was appointed, I passed the torch to another board member using the "volun-told" method I experienced a year prior. I passed off the box of historical information and went on to serve as president and past president in the following years. This experience taught me about building long-term, professional relationships. Through this organization, I connected with many other organizations as my career grew and expanded.

One of the biggest accomplishments I will credit to the New York State Cooperative and Experiential Education Association was my ability to get managerial experience. Before NYSCEEA, I had only managed one or two interns, but this experience allowed me to speak about manager-level experience in my interviews. I was able to call upon this experience in every interview when I pursued assistant director level roles. Serving as vice president meant I was responsible for mobilizing the organization to prepare for the annual conference. All the board members played a vital role in the organization's success and planning of the conference. There was no way I could have done that alone. I had to delegate, check in, and manage every piece to ensure a successful event. Through this organization, I also connected with professionals throughout New York State in city, state, and private universities, which helped elevate my career and network me into other professional associations and other job opportunities I would not have had otherwise.

This experience catapulted my career, and this is what I wish for you. It may not be a personal and professional development association that connects you with others, but you need to determine what will allow you to have a brand outside of your full-time job. Even if you worked in a job for

10 or 15 years, and this book is in your hand, I want you to think about expanding your brand outside of your current team, department, company, and institution. I am not asking you to leave your current job and prepare to make your next move your best move at another company, but this is a tactic to ensure you are prepared regardless of what your company or institution decides to do.

Remember, as a full-time, salaried employee, you are in most cases an "at-will" employee, and the company can let you go at any time. I've seen it time and time again, especially with COVID-19, when dedicated employees have put in good work with their head down, submitting assignments, and expanding the role to cover other team members and then they are let go with no place to go ultimately. If those same professionals had been building relationships and networking inside and outside of the company, they would have had relationships to lean on to help them navigate to the next level versus starting at ground zero and building their personal and professional brand while they were unemployed.

I ask you to dig deeper into your personal and professional brand. Think about your manifesto. What is your mission? What is your vision? How can you start communicating your mission and vision in the world of work?

Your Next Move

Your mission and vision are pivotal to how you talk about your personal and professional brand. *Your mission statement is the value you create and whom you create it for, plus the expected outcome.* Essentially, you are communicating the value you bring to the workforce and what someone can expect by working with you, similar to a properly written cover letter when you break down the experiences you've had that directly correlate to the job you're applying to. At the end of each paragraph, where you share your experiences, it's important to summarize your value by saying something like, "Based upon my experience doing (A), I would be able to do (B) if selected for this role."

One of my favorite mission statements is from Oprah Winfrey. In a *Fast Company* article, it noted her personal mission statement as "To be a teacher. To be known for inspiring my students to be more than they thought they can be."[1] When you think about Oprah Winfrey, you think about how she teaches people to live their best lives. She has used the aforementioned slogan for years. On *The Oprah Winfrey Show*, she brought countless guests, artists, entrepreneurs, teachers, and thought leaders to sit across from her on the stage and teach us how to live our best lives. She served as an objective teacher to share many topics, resources, and information to help her audience elevate their lives. If her mission is to be a teacher, I would say that she's 100% reached that milestone.

A mission statement, like the core values discussed in Chapter 3, is not necessarily two separate statements created to represent you at work and you at home. A mission statement is a combined way of articulating who you are overall.

When I think about the Manifest Yourself company manifesto, I know it aligns closely with my personal and professional values and what I would like to be known for in the workplace. The three core values I talk about from Manifest Yourself are excellence, resilience, and being a credible source for information. We exude excellence in everything we do, we are resilient and always prepared for the bounce back, and we are a credible source for personal and professional development information. I use "we" when speaking about my company, but I simply replace that with "I" when speaking about myself.

Manifest Yourself is a leadership development company providing tailor-made solutions to hire, develop, engage, and retain women and people of color. We utilize workshops, training programs, seminars, and consulting services to train companies and

---

[1] S. Vozza, "Personal Mission Statements of 5 Famous CEOs and Why You Should Write One Too," *Fast Company*, February 25, 2014. Retrieved January 10, 2020, from www.fastcompany.com/3026791/personal-mission-statements-of-5-famous-ceos-and-why-you-should-write-one-too.

organizations on hiring, developing, engaging, and retaining their people. With everything my company does, our goal is to promote community and excellence and support women and people of color looking to shatter glass ceilings in their respective industries. Those statements are closely tied to who I am as a professional and what I bring to the workforce.

So, for this next move, I want you to think about your mission and vision. What is your manifesto, and how does this connect to the workplace? You may look at this and say, "This seems very personal," but we can always go back and take out a little bit of information to make it connect more to the workplace. This is truly the experience you provide to anyone who interacts with you. Anyone who interacts with me as a professional knows I exude excellence, I am resilient, and I like to be a credible source. I do my best to always showcase that, and I want you to get super clear on your core values you exude that align closely to your mission and vision, and ultimately, your manifesto of who you are. This is a part of your personal and professional brand.

When we think about how this manifests itself in the workplace, you may not necessarily quote your mission, vision, or manifesto during an interview. This statement can be used in an elevator pitch, social media profiles, or a LinkedIn profile. These things are not separate entities. I want you to look closely at how these experiences come together and align with your overall personal and professional brand.

When we think about women and people of color in the workforce, we frequently talk about code switching, which is when you feel like you are one person at home and one person in the office. Today, what I'm asking you to do is merge these two people into one. Allow yourself to think about yourself holistically. Although this may be difficult, when you think about everything that comes together to make you the person you are today, and you start thinking about the companies and roles that align with all of you, you will ultimately have a lot more satisfaction in your day-to-day experience in the workplace. We spend 40-plus-hours a week in the office, so why not have a company and role that align with our mission, vision, and personal and professional brand and lead us to increased happiness?

Your core values: _____

_____

_____

_____

Your personal mission statement: _____

_____

_____

_____

Chapter 10

Embracing Your Voice in the Workplace

Career Affirmation: My unique voice is valued and needed in the workplace.

S tanding up for yourself in the workplace is an extremely important skill. We can determine your core values, talk about personal and professional branding, and get clear on so many elements of who you are, but if you can't stand up for who you are in the workplace, then none of that information will come to light. One of the important lessons I've learned over the past few years is the difference between sharing sentiments and the ability to execute.

In a conversation with a manager, I had expressed needing more time on an assignment that was just dropped on my desk. In a culture where everything is needed yesterday and not by the end of the week, it's easy to fall behind. In many of the recent roles I've held, I've been asked to develop the strategies that may be executed by my team or another team in the office. Most professionals responsible for building out strategies know they come together best when they have time to thoroughly explore the scenario's full scope and plan alternative solutions to ensure they're accounting for all of the variables.

As the day was coming to an end, I was asked to deliver something by the end of the same business day. The end of the day in this role could mean well after 9:00 p.m., but all the same, it needed to get done immediately. While I know I am generally able to put together something phenomenal on short notice based on my years of experience in the field, I also acknowledge that a little more time allows me to polish various attributes of the strategy that I wouldn't have necessarily thought of with my first draft going out as my final draft. This had happened multiple times throughout the summer with this manager, so I reached back out via email and said something along the lines of:

Not a problem. I will get this to you by the end of the day. However, I would greatly appreciate a bit more advance notice to think about this more thoughtfully versus putting something together today as a final draft. I know I'd be able to perfect this strategy with an additional 24 hours of notice before needing to submit the work.

Well, the manager replied and said something along the lines of:

You know the way our team works right now, and we just need to get things out. I need you to execute this as soon as possible. Being a team player is essential and working with aggressive timelines is a large part of our work. I sense a little bit of pushback here. I'd greatly appreciate us having a conversation.

I was livid.

I was beside myself because no matter the role, I always meet deadlines and ensure my team works to keep up, if not ahead, of timelines. Whether you tell me you need it in five minutes, an hour, a week, or two months, I always ensure timely completion. Throughout my career, I've always identified myself as a professional who never likes to be called out, meaning waiting for a senior leader or manager to realize that you didn't do something before actually doing the work. I pride myself on making sure that I get the work done before anyone asks for it. Even when I'm asked for something new on a tight deadline, I pride myself on delivering the highest quality of work with the information I have at that moment. I may not always get it perfect, but I do things to the best of my ability with the information and time I am given. This particular manager also had a bad habit of not reading emails in a timely manner, so often our team would have more aggressive deadlines because the original email with deliverables was finally shared the day the assignment was due versus the week prior when the original email was initially delivered with the ask.

When I reread the email from my supervisor, I was angry because while I was sharing sentiments about appreciating more time, the manager tied this to my capability to execute on the deadline and not being a team player. Sentiments versus execution

are different conversations. Sharing sentiments is essentially sharing your feelings about being able or unable or wishing you had
more of something versus execution, which is one's ability to do
the job. I would never share that I am unable to do something
unless that's truly the case.

I promptly responded to my manager, sharing that I had never
missed a deadline or failed to execute throughout my career at this
company. I was simply sharing that this had occurred multiple
times in a short period when assignments needed to be delivered
quickly, and I felt that if I had a little bit more time, I could provide
a more thorough strategy to the questions asked. This in no way
reflected my ability to do my job and not be a team player. If I'm
honest, I also wanted to share that there were several times that
summer where I'd worked longer hours to deliver something
"urgent" and the meeting was canceled, the strategy was never
reviewed, or there was an opportunity to ask for additional time
but the manager never bothered to ask for a 24-hour extension or
clarify what the deadline was instead of pushing the team to deliver
immediately. However, I reserved those sentiments for a virtual
happy hour conversation with a close friend and co-worker.

Years ago, I would have never advocated for myself in this way
and share that I would have appreciated more time. The only email
the manager would have received was an ask about what time was
considered the end of the day for this particular assignment to
ensure that I wrapped up my other projects or scraped my existing
schedule to reprioritize my new tasks. I would have simply done
the work, attempted to do my best while stressing myself out, and
submitted it by the end of the day.

Oddly enough, this tough conversation led to a wonderful,
deeper conversation during a midyear review that shared more
about both of our core values and strengths and why my manager
responded in the manner that they did. This was a conversation I
would have avoided years ago for fear of retaliation or being written up as a disgruntled colleague. I know it's imperative to speak
up, whether speaking up to a manager, skip leader, or senior

leadership, to allow my thoughts to be heard as they relate to the work I'm asked to put out into the company. Additionally, in my recent roles, I've had a team behind me, so I have to speak up for my team and not just for myself. But, this doesn't mean that speaking up is not a muscle that I've had to learn to exercise in the workplace.

As you move into senior-level roles, you will see that your work has even more impact. Early in my career, I was lucky if my work even reached the rest of my team and if my peers and senior management knew the work I was responsible for. I was working in a silo. *As you grow in your career, you will see that your work reaches farther than your desk and farther than your manager checking off to say that you completed or did not complete any given task. Your work can impact your colleagues, entire team, manager, and department, and ultimately have the power to impact the company.* The work I was doing in this role reached the executive leadership team, so I wanted to ensure that everything I submitted was well thought out.

With time, I knew my ideas would only become more developed, and I would catch mistakes and opportunities to improve the concepts presented. I realized I was fearful of "cancel culture." I was fearful of saying the wrong thing, not just for retaliation at the moment, but ultimately impacting my career trajectory. When working in a culture where relationships are pivotal, there can be a fear of saying the wrong thing, which turns into you and your brand being attached to saying the wrong thing. I always emphasize that if you work on articulating your ideas, strategies, and sentiments with grace and not from a place of anger, even though I was livid in that situation, "cancel culture" should not be a concern in most cases.

That summer, in another conversation with my work mentor, I realized that I experienced anxiety when I stretched myself in a way that I hadn't before. When I used my voice in a new way, it rattled me and made me question my ability to do my job, articulate my ideas, and fear how other leaders would view my abilities moving forward. I quickly learned that my ability, also known as my execution, is not necessarily correlated to my feelings. As one of my favorite personal mentors frequently says, "Feelings aren't facts." If you feel something, it doesn't necessarily mean it's real.

When I had that conversation in a frenzy with my work mentor and shared that I was worried about how people would perceive me if I went too far, she reassured me I was simply exercising my right to use my voice powerfully. It wasn't me being difficult or an "angry Black woman." It was me stretching to a new professional level. It was me leveling up and standing up for myself in new ways.

That same summer, I watched the movie *Mulan*, which was adapted as a non-animated film by Disney. I always reflect on the moment Mulan pretended to be a male in the army to protect the emperor. Every day, she hid her identity as a woman, and she hid her skill level to avoid unwanted attention from the other members of her unit. One day, she was called into the tent of the commanding officer, and he asked, "Why are you holding back? Your chi is strong. Why aren't you allowing people to see who you are? There's no need to hide and be like everyone else."[1]

When I think about my career and life, there are experiences that are unique to me. I've received opportunities that others have not because of who I am and my personal and professional brand. Every time, I leveled up to a new opportunity or I stretched myself to articulate an idea in a new way; I felt scared out of my mind. I would often catch myself "playing small" because I'm afraid to make a public mistake that I can't take back. Like Mulan, I know my chi is strong. Hell, you're reading an actual book that I've written that's published by a reputable publisher, and that's a feat in itself! And rather than openly acknowledge successes I've had in my business and career, I've often shrunk myself and minimized my experience, talents, and potential to ensure I don't appear "too big for my britches," as my dad would say – an old-school way of saying you're getting too full of yourself.

---

[1] J. Weiner, J. Reed, and C. Bender (Producers), N. Caro, (Director), *Mulan*, 2020 [television].

My television appearance on Sister Circle Live in the fall of 2019 was my first time on television, and it was *live* television. When preparing with my brand manager, I did not want them to know that it was my first time, so I didn't share with them or the network. Instead, I overprepared myself in every way possible to anticipate the questions of the host and producers. I watched countless episodes of the show to ensure I understood each host's temperaments and could anticipate the types of questions they would ask. I studied my interview topic inside and out and practiced questions from every angle. There was no free moment leading up to the show that I did not rehearse questions to ensure I would look natural on screen.

The television appearance went extremely well, and after it was over, I told my brand manager that I had never been on live television before. They were stunned. When my brand manager asked me why I didn't tell them, I explained that I thought if I told them it was my first time, they might say I wasn't ready and should practice on a smaller scale. I was fearful that by being new and in a situation that was foreign to me that someone would say, "Hey, maybe you should wait your turn." This has been a fear I've had for a long time in my business, but as any entrepreneur knows, every day you grow and scale, you experience new things. Many times, if you do not have a mentor, teacher, or coach to lead you, you've got to figure it out alone. You must learn to rise to the occasion. In this instance, I was rising due to having a scarcity mindset. I rose to the occasion, but deep down, I also feared it would be taken away if I told the truth. I have a track record of rising to the occasion, so I wasn't necessarily worried that I would make a fool of myself on network television. Instead, I was afraid that someone wouldn't believe I was ready since I hadn't done it before.

I've learned time and time again that using your voice may not be easy, but it's needed. Advocating for yourself in the workplace is similar to growing a muscle. Each time you go to the gym, you're training your body to get stronger. If you haven't been to the gym in a long time, those first few sessions can make you feel like you made a huge mistake, but over time you start to see results. Exercises that you attempted on your first day in the gym will be much easier during your workout a month later. That same exercise probably won't even make you break a sweat six months later. In the same way you may work out and lift heavier weights or try more challenging movement, you'll need to do the same thing when you advocate for yourself in the workplace.

When something doesn't feel right to you, that's an indication that it may be time to speak up. *It's natural to feel nervous, fearful, or even doubt that you should be speaking up at all! But, think of the possibilities that can happen as a result of speaking up for yourself.* Very early in my career when I worked a full-time job and waited tables in the evenings, advocating for myself looked like telling my manager that I couldn't "close the restaurant" during the week. Since I had to be up so early to commute into the New York City from Long Island, I knew I needed to leave the restaurant by 9 p.m. I didn't want to risk my productivity at my full-time job by closing the restaurant and not getting home until after 1 a.m. during the week. I remember feeling so nervous to have the conversation, and there definitely was some pushback, but I was able to advocate for the schedule that I needed.

As I moved into more senior roles in career development, advocating for myself looked more like negotiating my salary, starting conversations about needing more resources, or disagreeing with the way to approach a project. Each time I stood up for myself, it confirmed my own ability to advocate for myself. When you practice in situations that are smaller, it also helps you prepare for larger conversations like negotiating your salary or standing up for injustices in the workplace.

While I cannot promise that the conversations will be easy or that the person on the other end of the conversation will be eager to have the conversation too, I can promise you that advocating for yourself is like keeping a promise to yourself. You're promising that you will always act in your best interest to ensure that you're able to navigate the workplace in alignment with your core values. This isn't about being selfish or ignoring the needs of others; it's about identifying problems that you know should be addressed. And if you're a manager, there's also the need for you to advocate for yourself and your team! In many scenarios, your team may be looking to you for leadership and advocacy in rooms they may not be in with you.

Your Next Move

Your next move for this chapter will be short, but I want you to reflect on the times in your career when you did not stand up for yourself. I call these your do-better moments. Think of three to five times you did not stand up for yourself in the workplace and the commonalities in each scenario. Did you not stand up for yourself because you were among a large group of people and did not want to raise your voice a bit to make sure you were heard? Were you in a room with a chatty Cathy, and you allowed her to articulate her ideas instead of yours or were you one-on-one with a leader who you felt had the power to change the trajectory of your career for better or for worse? I want you to think about those moments and write what you wish you could have articulated during that time. Write out the way you wanted to share your ideas, strategies, and sentiments. Moving forward, when in similar situations, I challenge you to speak up.

One of the keys I would like to share is that sometimes we need to practice before we speak up. Do not go into a situation unprepared, only to realize it's an unfamiliar, heated environment. Many times, if you don't speak up at the moment, you can still reach out the next day when you feel like you can articulate yourself better and share your ideas, strategies, and sentiments in a way that best represents you. It's okay if you need some time. However, I challenge you to be timely.

Like an interview that doesn't go as smoothly as planned, I tell my clients to never walk out of the interview and just say, "Well, I messed up. Guess this isn't the job for me." *If you know you messed up in your interview, I challenge you to write a thank you note and address wherever you messed up. Acknowledge that you may not have articulated your answers and share what you would have said.* Standing up for yourself is not always in the context of a potential argument or situation gone bad. Standing up for yourself involves any situation that you feel deserves your insights, clarification, and support. The same thing goes for some of these tough situations or do-better moments in the workplace. *If you know you may need a bit of time and you did not miss the boat by waiting, take a second to address the situation properly. Over time, you will be able to build up your "courage muscle."* As Brené Brown says, "Vulnerability is courage." Standing up for yourself is being vulnerable. Building up the courage to stand up for yourself will take time. Revealing vulnerability is like building a muscle. Every moment you stand up for yourself, you will become more comfortable day after day, week after week, month after month, and year after year. More importantly, you will begin to get comfortable owning your professional power, sharing your skill set, and articulating what's important to you in every role, regardless of the particular situation. Use the section below to reflect on your do-better moments.

Do-better moment: _____

_____

_____

_____

Do-better moment: _____

_____

_____

_____

Do-better moment: _____

_____

_____

_____

Do–better moment: _____

_____

_____

_____

Do–better moment: _____

_____

_____

_____

Commonalities or key themes in your do-better moments: _____

_____

_____

_____

Listing commonalities is important to ensure you preemptively recognize these moments going forward and work to prepare yourself to speak up adequately. When you can identify situations in which you ignore your core values or you see yourself shrinking to avoid a conversation, those are indicators that advocating for yourself and others may be needed.

Chapter 11

The Truth about Salary Negotiation

Career Affirmation: I am worthy of a salary that reflects my skills and experience.

I n the previous chapter, we dug into how to stand up for your- self, and we focused on having those tough conversations when you recognize an opportunity to say something mean- ingful or provide critical feedback in the workplace. In this chap- ter, it's time to talk about getting to the money.

Yes, I'm talking about salary negotiation.

The truth about salary negotiation is that it's much more closely tied to your personal and professional brand than you may think. Often, clients hire me to prepare them for that final conver- sation when the recruiter or hiring manager extends a final offer for the role they've been interviewing for. I jokingly call this the battle. Many professionals focus on this conversation like they are preparing for battle. They expect a lowball offer that does not reflect what they want, but what if we flip the script and set the expectation that the company will already be giving you a great offer and your responsibility is only to negotiate the cherry on top?

Salary negotiation conversations are less about that final conversation and more about (a) positioning yourself as a leader in your industry from the moment the company interacts with you, so they automatically provide you with a solid offer; and (b) reiterating your personal and professional brand, accomplishments, and professional track record of success during "the battle" to ensure your request for an increase is validated by your experience versus your desire for a higher offer. This isn't only about asking for more money because you need it. This conversation's focus is based on your results, track record, and promise to continue to produce high-quality work to impact the company if you accept the negotiated offer.

By now, we know many statistics about women in the work- force. Women frequently earn less than men for performing work of equal value. The gender pay gap still exists for women when compared to men of the same race or ethnicity. Additionally, in an article from Bloomberg[1] on female CFOs, it noted that they

---

[1] J. Green, and S. Basak "Female CFOs Brought in $1.8 Trillion More Than Male Peers," Bloomberg, October 16, 2019. Retrieved March 1, 2020, from www.bloomberg.com/ news/articles/2019-10-16/female-cfos-brought-in-1-8-trillion-more-than-male-peers.

brought in $1.8 trillion more than their male peers. "Within the first 24 months of appointing female CFOs, companies saw, on average, a 6% increase in profits and an 8% better stock return, compared to the performance of male predecessors."[2]

When I think about salary negotiation, I recognize this is less about that number you get in the moment and more about the lifetime of a career. Whether you are a male or female reading this book, when you do not negotiate your salary, it equates to a lifetime of loss, not just on the wages earned, but on losing out on having more funds for food and housing, childcare, decreased retirement savings, paying off student loans and other debt, and your overall quality of life, whether that's real estate, cars, travel, or whatever it is that you are interested in.

Let's review my three-step process for helping you negotiate a higher salary.

Step 1: Assessing your value as a professional

Are you comfortable articulating your professional value? Basically, are you able to articulate your personal and professional brand in conversations before, during, and after the interview process? When I think about the early days of my career, I look back at that picture of my mom and dad from a student-affairs awards dinner. I was winning an award for my contribution to the university. I was so happy in this photo. I had just walked in a fashion show at my university. I had a long, flowy weave in my hair, and I was wearing a cute dress (I have no idea where it is now). Mom and Dad were suited, booted, and smiling, so excited about what I would do upon graduation in May. In this photo, I see the hope for what was to come in my life after graduation.

At that time, I knew I had one more class to complete at a community college nearby, but behind my smile, my mind was

---

[2] Ibid.

spinning. I had no idea what I brought to the table. I did not know anything about my skills or how to articulate my experiences, and I had no idea how to determine if I was the best fit for a role. I was more focused on simply needing to graduate and walk across that stage … and make money, so I didn't have to move back to Connecticut with my parents. Oh, and I was focused on paying my student loans back within six months. The feeling I had in 2008 as a fresh graduate from undergrad studies is similar to the feeling many professionals have when they have 3, 5, and sometimes 10 years of experience, but are not clear on their skills and how they bring those skills to the workforce.

The first step in assessing your value is taking stock of your career, thinking about every job you've had, every employer you've worked for, and the acquired skills and competencies you gained as a direct result of working at that company. Hint, hint – we did this together in Chapter 2. Frequently, you may also hear professionals refer to this as transferable skills. *Transferable skills are the skills and competencies you've gained from one role that will help you in your next role.* An example of a transferable skill would be presentation skills. If you've presented your work at one company, that's a skill you would be able to bring with you to another company. Although you may need to get up to speed on the company's presentation style or format, it would not be your first time presenting, so you already have the foundation. It's extremely important to think about your skills as they relate to the roles you experienced, but also as your skills relate to you being in the world of work.

For example, in one of my first jobs after undergrad, as mentioned earlier, I worked as a marketing analyst at an office supply company in New York City. When I reflect on this experience, I quickly remember that I hated this job. I spent hours doing all types of data entry for various products I had no interest in, and I assembled the pricing structure for customers I did not know. I expected this job to be more aligned with my Shanté and Conny dreams of developing campaigns and creating print and digital ads. I was not interested in any type of data entry. When I think about this job, I never spoke about the skills I gained because until I became more seasoned in my career, I did not believe that this experience gave me any skills. However, when I thought objectively about this experience, I realized I learned how a company could tier its pricing based on the relationship it had with every customer. I learned more about the sales of its clients and what was considered good and bad; what made the customer valued in the top tier, rather than a middle tier; and how the business adjusted appropriately based on the relationship that it had with each customer. This was not something I would have learned in a classroom setting. When I thought objectively and pulled out the skills I gained instead of my feelings, I realized how to leverage this experience in the future.

If you are unsure about your skills, it may be helpful to take a career assessment. Although there are many different assessments out there, I challenge you to think more objectively about each experience discussed in Chapter 2. Reflect on the projects, assignments, and tasks you completed and what you learned from them, regardless of whether you liked those tasks. Think about those skills as they relate to your brand. I like to call that your toolkit. *Your toolkit is your "bag of tricks" to bring with you from one job to another. When speaking about your bag, we are not referring to negative baggage and past mistakes. Instead, we are referring to your bag of experiences and transferable skills to apply to your new role based on your past experiences.* This toolkit helps you articulate your value in an elevator pitch, your resume and cover letters, and on LinkedIn and other social media platforms, and, ultimately, helps you leverage this bag of skills in your interview and salary negotiation conversations.

The toolkit is closely tied to your ability to negotiate a higher salary during these conversations. It doesn't matter what you believe your offer should look like if it's not based on your research of what the market pays for a role and the value that the company will receive from hiring you. *Your toolkit and personal and professional brand are reasons a company should hire you.*

Step 2: Understanding the value of the role and benefits

Your worth is what comparatively qualified people in your field are worth and maybe a bit more. In this step, it's time to understand what the market is paying for the role you are applying to by identifying comparable job titles and salary ranges for your geographic area, similar to the process of purchasing a home. Before you make an offer on a property or complete the home appraisal process, your realtor will pull "comps," which are homes in the area that are a similar size, location, and with similar features. When making an offer, it's generally a rule of thumb that if the home is comparable to other homes in the area, then the offer should be in alignment with the comps provided. If there is something unique about the home such as updated kitchen, bathrooms, or an extra feature, then your offer should be a bit higher than the comps in the area. Likewise, your salary offer should be comparable to similar titles, roles, and companies in the immediate area.

The first place I love to go to begin research is LinkedIn. LinkedIn has a tool to research the roles you are interested in and the salary range based on your geographic area. By the way, you will make more in a metropolitan area like New York City or San Francisco versus a more remote area with fewer company headquarters. There are certain markets based on the cost of living where you will make more money, and that must be considered as you evaluate salaries.

You may also notice a lack of opportunities in your geographic area. I've worked with clients who were very passionate about working in a particular field, but as they researched jobs, they noticed there were not many roles available in their area. Better yet, they discovered that the types of companies they always dreamed of were not available in their geographic area. This may be a sign to consider moving if you have dreams of working in a certain industry that is not prevalent in your current city. With COVID-19, many people are not working in a physical office, but many companies still have plans of bringing their workforce back into the office in some capacity in the future. By the time this book is in your hands, it may be a whole different story, but as of late 2020/early 2021, many companies are committed to returning to the office regularly with reduced capacity sometime in mid to late 2021.

As you research salaries, remember to look at different titles. Titles are subjective, so it's important to consider the norms of the company. For example, as assistant director of admissions, I quickly noticed there was not a role below assistant director at the institution that I worked for during my transition from financial services to higher education in 2010. There were senior assistant directors, associate directors, senior associate directors, and the department head who was a director. Upon reaching out to a few contacts and conducting online research, I learned that this college elevated the admissions counselor title to assistant director. The responsibilities matched other admissions counselor roles in the area; it was just elevated. Consequently, when I conducted additional research and compared salaries, I compared the role I was seeking as an assistant director to other admissions counselor roles in the area. There are many different, creative titles that companies use to describe the same types of work, so it's important to research and understand what titles are closely related to the job you are seeking so that you can benchmark all of those job titles and ultimately come up with a target salary range.

The range may be large, but the next step is finding out your range based on your skill set and years of experience. Outside of LinkedIn, I also incorporate data from Glassdoor, PayScale, and a basic Google search to ensure I am fully informed of the full range for the role in my geographic area. For example, through your research, you may find that the full range of compensation is $55,000 to $110,000. However, you should never quote this number to a hiring manager or recruiter. *It's best to quote a range of $10,000 to $15,000; you never want to quote such an ambiguous range* *that the company cannot understand your actual salary expectations.* When you look at the skills required, your experience level, and considering the geographic area that this role takes place, maybe your range will be $75,000 to $90,000.

At this time, it's also important to consider your budget. You must ensure you can live your life, pay your bills, and cover other mandatory expenses or things you deem important. Understanding a realistic budget is essential to the process. So, while the market pays a certain amount based on the role, it's also important to consider if you can afford to live on that salary range. It goes without saying, but you should not communicate your budget in an interview.

I've spent much of my career working and living in the Greater New York area, and I have clients who come to me and say, "I need to make at least $100,000 to live in New York City. My budget, my rent, my kids...." However, that does not matter when you are having a salary negotiation conversation. Your budget is what I like to call the "behind closed doors information." You know what you need to make to live in the manner you would like to live, but that is not something you should communicate during any career-related conversation when you are negotiating your salary or a raise. You will know this information and ensure that your requested salary range, matched with your level of experience, is what you use to inform the range you're requesting. *During the actual conversation, you will focus on your skills, experiences, and accomplishments to advocate for a salary that reflects the work you've done throughout your career and the value you will bring to the company.*

Once you determine your target salary range, I also recommend determining your "hell-no" number for the role. The hell-no number is the number you cannot accept based on your budget and level of experience. In conversations with any company, it's important to know when you'd walk away from the offer because you (a) cannot afford to live on that salary or (b) you believe the salary is not a reflection of your experience, skills, and value you would be bringing to the company. It's a personal decision to walk away from an offer, but if you are truly not compensated in a manner that represents your experience, and the benefits of taking the role do not outweigh that, it might be time to walk away.

Earlier in my career, I took a $20,000 pay cut because I knew that the industry I was moving into didn't pay in the same manner as my current industry. Unless I could come in at a much higher level, which I was not qualified to do, a pay cut was my only option. At the time, my expenses were high, but I opted to redo my budget to accommodate the role because I wanted to make this transition. I know many professionals who would say, "There ain't no way I'm taking a $20,000 pay cut," but in less than three years, I made up for it with a $20,000 salary increase. Then I more than doubled that initial salary offer in about six years when I transitioned into another role. For me, it made sense, and I knew it was a temporary salary reduction that would ultimately lead to a long-term career path that genuinely excited me.

When discussing your hell-no number, it's also important to consider the new role's benefits. Although benefits may not add additional funds to your bank account, they may lower your cost of living in addition to providing you with a much needed professional experience. Often, we focus so much on that bottom dollar amount that we forget there are other items to negotiate or benefits to gain for working at that company that may significantly and positively impact your life. These are especially important, especially when the company cannot meet your salary requirements. Benefits like vacation time, sick time, medical insurance, stock options, matching retirement contributions, transportation assistance, gym reimbursement, tuition assistance, student loan assistance, parking/travel benefits, and a sign-on bonus can all add up to dramatically impact your life. Pre-COVID-19, benefits like transportation and parking assistance can make a huge difference when working in a metropolitan area. You may feel like you are making a bit more because you aren't spending as much to get to work each day.

Early in my career, when I was looking at career opportunities and making my first transition to career development, one of the greatest impacts on my salary was no longer traveling across a bridge to get to my office. When I looked at the salary I wanted to receive, I knew if I stayed on the side of the bridge where I lived, I could actually afford a different salary range because I was no longer paying a large amount of money for transportation. This isn't to say that you should negotiate less than you feel reflects your level of experience or less than market value, but this may work in your favor if you are moving to a new industry where the salary is lower and you're also able to lower personal expenses.

Another major benefit is tuition assistance. If you would like to go back to school and earn another degree or certification and the company has a great tuition assistance program, that significant benefit can catapult your career into a new role and use that for future roles. *As a reminder, from the moment you have a conversation with a recruiter or hiring leader, you should be prepared to talk about everything except the company's benefits.* Recruiters often ask about salary range when you get on the call as part of the screening process to ensure you are on the same page. No one wants to start interviewing for a job and learn that the salary range is not close to what he or she was expecting and there's no room to negotiate. Once you receive an actual offer, you can ask for the full benefits package if you haven't already found it on the company website.

Again, the salary negotiation process begins the moment you interact with the company. When you know you are ready for change, make sure to do the research on comparable roles and determine the parts of your professional toolkit before you start applying for jobs, or, better yet, get invited to apply from someone in your network. This is similar to when you are looking to purchase a real estate property. When you are close to making an offer on a new home, one of the first things you should do is look at the purchase price in comparison to homes that recently sold in the area. You want to ensure that the offer you are about to make is on target, not too low and not too high.

Step 3: Have a strategy to approach the salary negotiation conversation

You need to plan and implement a strategy for all salary conversations. *You will see the word "strategy" throughout this book because it's important to stop relying on chance and start making informed decisions related to your career. This is your career that you are building. The power is not only in the company's hands; it's in your hands, too.* I always share with my clients that interview and salary negotiation conversations are a two-way street. As much as the company is interviewing you to determine if they would like to hire you, you are also interviewing the company and every employee you interact with to see if you would like to accept an offer with the company as well.

Practice having skill-based and accomplishment-based conversations that ultimately drive the interviewers to understand the value you would bring if selected to work at that company. The No. 1 tip I share about salary negotiation is never to accept the first offer on the phone. *Never!* You lose most of your negotiating power if you get too excited and immediately say yes. Share your excitement if you know you will most likely accept the offer, but always ask for 24 to 48 hours and request to see the full benefits package so you can make an informed decision or plan to negotiate the salary and additional benefits.

If you are interviewing for other jobs at the same time, this is the time to ask the other companies when they will be making a decision on your candidacy. In these situations, you would reach out to the other companies you are interviewing to understand where you are in the process if you do not already know and inquire about their timeline of making a decision. You will want to be timely on both fronts, but if you are not toward the end of the other company's interview process, this may be a bit difficult.

Again, exceptions can be made for greatness, so the other company may do its best to expedite its hiring process by moving up interview schedules or extending an offer if it does not want to lose you. If you know you will not accept the offer you have in front of you, go back to those other companies and ask them when they feel they will decide. It's a delicate balance to ensure you advocate for yourself while communicating with all parties involved. *The world is smaller than you think, so do not be surprised if you interview or connect with the same colleagues when making another career move. I never recommend handling a situation like this lightly and ruining a relationship with a recruiter or hiring leader during this phase in the game.* They may just pop up as a key stakeholder in another interview down the line.

Even if you have only one offer, you should respond in a timely manner. Throughout all of this, it's imperative to practice, practice, and practice some more so you are prepared for the various conversations that may come your way during this phase. *Being underprepared can be detrimental to your personal and professional brand and your overall career.*

Last but certainly not least, whether you negotiate your salary for a new role or a raise in your current job, remember to ask for what you want versus what you think you can get. If you back your salary conversation with your skills, experience, and accomplishments, and not just based on your ideas or what you've seen your friends get, you will start with a strong foundation. *This is not about what you think you can get; it's about what you deserve to be compensated for the work you bring and the experience you will provide as an employee at that company.*

Before we move into the "Your Next Move" section, it's very important to address the scenario when you quote a specific salary range with the recruiter in the initial phone screening, but you learn that the role has more responsibilities and you'd like to change your target salary range once you receive an offer. Generally, it's in poor taste to push for a significantly higher salary when a company shares an offer on the higher end of the range you quoted in your initial interview. In the same way you want to confirm that your salary range is within the company's range, the company is also doing the same thing.

It's one thing to negotiate to ensure you're on the higher end of the initially quoted range, but it's a very different conversation when you're looking to negotiate significantly higher than the preestablished range in the earlier phase of the interview process. That's why it's so important to do your research before having any conversations with the company to know if your salary expectations are aligned with what you need. For example, if you have to move to a new state, those funds to move should be included in the salary range you quote, or you should ask if the company will assist with moving expenses in the initial conversations.

The one scenario when it is always appropriate to change your initial salary expectations is when you notice that the role's scope is significantly larger than it was noted in the job description and subsequent interviews with your future team's hiring manager and team members. In this case, when you receive an offer that is within the originally quoted range that you no longer feel is appropriate, it's important to speak to the additional responsibilities and quote a new salary range. *This isn't the time to simply state that you need more money; you always need to base your salary negotiation conversation on the benchmarking for comparable roles in the area, the value you will bring to the company, and your direct past experiences, and in this case, the expansion of the role and responsibilities.* Upon receiving the offer letter, ask for 24 to 48 hours to review the offer and the company benefits. Return to the conversation with your new target salary range that better reflects the expanded responsibilities and experience you bring to the company. In some companies and professions, this may be a time to discuss a sign-on bonus if you are truly interested in the role and know you'll be able to negotiate a salary increase in one to two years to make up for the initial, smaller salary.

Your Next Move

I invite you to go back into the three steps and determine if this is your time to begin a job search or have a performance conversation with your supervisor to understand if you are ready for a promotion. Negotiating a salary increase for a new internal role and an external role are very similar. The main difference is that some companies have policies on how much of an increase internal colleagues can receive when moving from one internal role to another. This is something that you can speak to your human resources team or recruiter to better understand.

If you are ready, start initiating conversations to articulate the value you bring and what role you want. If you are currently conflicted about whether you should pursue a role outside of the company or pursue a promotional opportunity at your current company, take some time to reflect on the current landscape of your role and industry. Confirm your next steps and ensure they align with your short-term and long-term goals discussed in Chapter 4 and Chapter 7.

In some companies, it can be easy to speak to your manager, have a conversation about your performance, and get promoted or receive a raise. In other companies, getting a promotion or a raise means a significant change to your title, which may be harder to negotiate. I still believe that exceptions can always be made for high performers who bring their best and drive results at a company. So, again, go for what you really want, not for what you think you can get. It's important to understand the landscape when going into these conversations so you are not unprepared, which could hurt your career much more than it would help. If you know you are ready to have these conversations right now, use the template below to help you prepare for the conversations in addition to the skills we spoke about in the "Your Next Move" section of Chapter 2.

Title/role you are seeking: _____

Total salary range from your research: _____

Your target salary range: _____

Your hell-no number: _____

Your ideal benefits package: _____

Your unique value proposition: _____

Last, write your script to have a basic outline of how you would like to approach the conversation. For many of my clients, we work to create a brief "career profile" presentation deck that may or may not be shared with the hiring manager. This career profile presentation includes an overview of your professional experiences, highlights key skills that are essential in the role that you currently possess, key accomplishments and accolades, testimonials, and, for more senior employees, it can include key initiatives or action plans that would be implemented if selected for the role. This is generally no more than five to seven slides. Even if the presentation is never shared, it's a great exercise to help synthesize your own thoughts and drive home how you will position yourself for the new role or salary increase.

As for your script, you do not need to read it word for word, but it's helpful to have key statements that speak to your unique value and preestablished sentences, including the target salary range you would like to receive. Sometimes, one of the hardest things to overcome in salary negotiation conversations is exuding confidence when stating the salary you would like to receive and why.

It goes without saying that these conversations can be difficult, but it's important for you to take the feelings out of the conversation and focus on the facts about the expertise that you're bringing to the table. Fear is the No. 1 reason people don't ask for a raise or negotiate salary. There are only three potential outcomes when you ask for more money: They could say yes, not now, or no. That's it. Those are the only options. Instead of being afraid to take this bold step. Ask yourself, "What is there to be afraid of?" The worst that could happen is that they say "no." This often helps to keep everything in perspective and take the pressure off of asking.

Prior to every salary negotiation conversation, I always ask my clients to reflect upon their "wins" in the workplace. *If you don't know what your wins are, this may be the perfect time to start making a "win list." A win list is a list of all of your professional accomplishments or career highlights that you can easily reflect upon.* I recommend having a running list on your personal computer so you don't lose the information if you move to another company, and having a folder in your inbox of your current job. Remember, your wins stay with you regardless of the company or role you are currently in.

Your win list can include accomplishments like improving upon a process that saved the company time or money, times that you were given a task and you achieved amazing results, ways that you seamlessly took on more responsibilities, or anything that showcases how you've brought value into your work and company. I also recommend keeping emails in your work inbox to remind you of when you've received positive feedback from your managers or peers. This is a wonderful reminder for yourself and a great addition to the salary negotiation conversation; not only are you adding value to the workplace in a meaningful way that warrants a salary increase, but you also have documented testimonials from your peers and managers.

Taking a moment to review your accomplishments and feedback right before a conversation is also a wonderful way to pump up your own self-esteem as well. Sometimes you need to remind yourself that you've done the work and you deserve the pay that you're requesting. *You're not asking for a salary increase because you simply want to make more money; you're asking for a salary increase because of the value you currently bring and the value you will continue to bring to the organization.*

Chapter 12

How to Know When It's Time to Go

Career Affirmation: I can walk away from a job or company that no longer serves me.

I could not write this book without discussing the right time to walk away from a job. Not every opportunity is a great one. This may be an unpopular opinion that perfectly fits into the "millennial mindset" that many other generations frown upon, but I'm going to say it anyway: You don't have to stick it out. If you are unhappy, feel like your growth is being stunted, or learn there is a proverbial glass ceiling at your job that does not support your growth, you do not have to stay. Like Jim Rohn once said, "If you don't like how things are, change it! You're not a tree." Sometimes, leaving a job can seem like an easy decision. *However, I want you to be strategic and allow this to be a conscious decision, not just because you are frustrated, feel underemployed, undervalued, and underappreciated, which are all valid reasons, but because you are consciously choosing to embark on a job search to ultimately find a career for yourself, rather than just another job.*

Before some folks tear me to shreds for encouraging you to leave your job, I will share that I believe it's important to exhaust your options and have a strategic career conversation before leaving. I also do not advocate leaving a job before you have another one lined up unless it's an extremely dire circumstance or you have six months to a year's worth of savings and you like playing Russian Roulette. Before submitting your letter of resignation, it's important to have honest conversations about your career trajectory with your manager or skip leader.

- Ask for feedback about your performance from your manager or skip leader.
- Understand the trajectory of your career at your current company.
- Understand the current climate of your industry and how that would impact a job search at that time.
- Ensure you have built strategic relationships with mentors and sponsors who can advocate for your next career move, regardless of whether it is internal or external to your current company.

Before making a career move, I stress to my clients that the work needs to begin *well before* any moves are made. This theory is one of the main reasons that I wanted to write this book! *Too often, we try to fast track the next move because we've reached a certain place in the current role where we feel we can no longer be happy.* If you are already at that place and know it's time to go, I will not advocate for you to stay.

It wasn't until I was preparing for my fourth professional move that I felt myself make a truly strategic career decision. Earlier I had shared that I was performing well – basically overperforming. I was also in classes to complete my Master of Science in counseling that required an external internship, all while innovating various ideas and strategies that the career-development office was working toward executing. I exceeded my goals, but my manager felt I had untapped potential and could further exceed my goals. It goes without saying that I was pissed. I was angry beyond measure. I had worked so hard that year. I could not understand why I was not being promoted when others in the office received promotions while doing less work and made fewer contributions to the office than I had in the past year.

At that moment, I felt that I had to take control of my career versus waiting to be recognized and provide an opportunity to myself. Women and people of color often wait to be recognized as high performers to be promoted and rise to the next level in an organization. I want you to switch that mode of thinking. *You can create a career that rewards you with opportunities, rather than waiting for someone in your current company to tap you on your shoulder and indicate it's time for you to rise.* This is why having this book in your hands is so important. We need tactics in our careers, so we know what to do.

This was the first time I felt like I truly made a strategic move in my career and not just moving because I was unhappy or simply believed my time had come to an end with a certain employer. I was performing at an organization, doing work that I thought was meaningful, and was excited to continue to excel as a leader in the industry. I had to sit back and think, "How can I grow my career in the same field but just not at this organization?"

It's essential to understand when it's time to leave and assemble a career strategy that allows you to be ready at all times. *You should always have options, even if you are happy in a job. Options don't always have to look like a way out either.* Each new relationship you build may provide you with options. Each task you complete in your career strategy may provide you with new possibilities. Each time you add a new skill to your toolkit, you are creating an option. That is why developing a career strategy is so important. Logging into your work computer each day with your head down, hoping that change will happen, is the farthest thing from an option. If you are on the fence about embarking on a job search, there are several reasons that you may think it's your time to go. Let's examine the seven most common reasons that may serve as signals to either start your job search to get a new job or have a serious conversation about getting promoted or increasing your current responsibilities.

1. ***Suddenly feeling bored at work:*** I'm not talking about being bored on a particular assignment or if things are slow in the office and you find yourself doing more online shopping than working. I'm talking about that feeling of being bored to your core, and you feel like you are still exceeding the organization's goals, but your mind craves more. The example I like to give is about a mother's feeling that her child needs more learning opportunities. She can see that her child has an aptitude for more, and she looks for additional books and resources, or it's time for her child to go to school even though he or she is only three and not ready to go to preschool. Moms talk about seeing the "light bulb" turn on in their child and knowing they need to do more for them because watching *Frozen* for the 28th time will not cut it. The same goes for your career. If you are bored beyond belief because you've mastered your role, and this boredom is also causing overall dissatisfaction, the time has come for you to think about your next move.

2. *You have been there for a while, but you feel like you finally started to outgrow your work*: If you've accomplished all there is to accomplish in your position, and you begin to feel constrained by your title and role, it may be time to start looking for options. Maybe you need to have a discussion with your manager about a power lateral or promotional opportunity, or maybe it's time to start looking at job boards if you know upward movement is not a possibility for you in your current company. The key is knowing you have done all you could do within the constraints of the role you currently hold.

3. *If you put in the time, but the pay still isn't where it should be:* Maybe you negotiated to the best of your ability, but two solid years have passed, and you are a consistent, high performer, yet you have not received more than a cost of living increase. The key is ensuring you put time into your role and you're performing well because you cannot complain about a pay level you accepted when you were hired, especially when you haven't put in enough time to showcase your professional value. Once you have been in a job for at least a year, observed how the business operates year-round, and you've mastered your job, it's more than acceptable to start looking for money inside and outside of your company. *However, having the experience and impact to back that desire to increase your salary is essential.* Many professionals have had a situation in which they quickly said "yes," and were excited about a job opportunity but realize they would be underpaid but that is not enough in this case.

4. *Having a conflict in the office that is not fixable:* This is tough. Sometimes, conflicts at work are difficult to navigate. If you've had a conflict with a manager or co-worker that is truly affecting your ability to perform in your job, then you may want to consider your options. However, I am a huge advocate for making sure you find a job before leaving your current job. It also helps to develop relationships with other colleagues to make sure you are guaranteed a quality recommendation, if needed. There are many types of conflicts that can happen in

the office. It goes without saying that if it's impacting your work, your ability to continue contributing, or someone is retaliating against you, you must go through the proper channels, generally through your human resources office, to document and share this. However, there may come a time when it may be best to either leave the department or leave the company to pursue your next role in an environment that supports your growth.

5. *You work for a department or company you do not like:* There is no use in working for a department or company that you cannot stand to be in for 40-plus hours per week. If you know you do not support the mission, the vision, or the work you are completing every day, it may be time to leave. Even if the economy may not be great or you feel as though the job you are looking for may be hard to come by, this must be a strategic move. Do not just pack up and quit today. Start applying for positions in other departments in your current company that could make you happy or at a new company that you feel aligns with your career strategy and has what you need to thrive. *When it comes to making career decisions, consider everything involved – the people, company, your work, and the trajectory you will have when doing this work.* All those factors come into play.

6. *Circumstances in your personal life make your job harder:* Changes in your personal life can be even harder if your job is making it more difficult. Maybe you got married and with your spouse bought a house that is super far from work. Maybe you were thinking of starting a family and know your office could care less about work-life balance for its employees. Maybe you have a health concern, and the long hours and late nights in the office won't allow you to care for yourself properly. Maybe COVID-19 significantly impacted your responsibilities for your family and you need to reevaluate your work situation. Those are all valid reasons, and there are probably hundreds more, that can make it time for you to start thinking about navigating and building a career that supports your

current life stage. Evaluate whether you can do anything to stay at your current job if you would like to stay, such as reduced hours, an alternative schedule, or a permanent remote arrangement. Still, if your current job does not fit your lifestyle, it may be time to think about leaving.

7. *You've found out there's a glass ceiling at your company:* If you've hit a glass ceiling at your job, and you know there is no possible way for you to get promoted, develop further, and reap any of the benefits that that company provides, you may need to explore outside opportunities where you can spread your wings. One of my favorite quotes is from Dr. Barbara Ross Lee, a nationally recognized expert on health policy issues. Dr. Lee spoke at a women's leadership dinner when I was pursuing my bachelor's degree, and she said, "When you feel that you've hit a glass ceiling, find a bigger room." There is always the option to take your next move outside of the company.

There are many reasons outside of those seven, but it's important to know that only you will know when the time has come to go. To make your next move your best move, I encourage you to be strategic. It goes without saying that sometimes you are trying to leave, but things just aren't connecting.

Before I looked to transition my career back into corporate America, I was looking for a director-level job in higher education. I was always coming up as the second candidate in my interview processes and ultimately I was not selected for the job. For one particular job I was very interested in, I had over four rounds of interviews at the university, including a 60-minute presentation at which I delivered strategies to improve the office environment and revamp the office to ensure success. I also interviewed with the university president about what I was looking to create for the students, faculty, and alumni who frequently use the office of career services. I felt that, because of my history with the university, this job was going to be mine. However, as you can imagine from this story, I did not get selected for the role, and I was devastated.

There have been very few times in my career when I was so upset that I shed tears about not getting an opportunity, and this was one of them. I had already envisioned myself with the new commute into the office. I even envisioned the trench coat I was going to wear on my first day to the office, too. I was so close I could taste it.

Oddly enough, a little over a week after I was informed that I did not get the job, the No. 1 candidate rescinded their acceptance, and the university reached back out to me. At first, I thought this was fate. The candidate had found a nuance in the benefits package and could no longer accept the offer, so the hiring manager reached back out to me. We had a great conversation about my sincere interest in the university and the role, and I confirmed that I would still be delighted to accept the offer. As a final step, already knowing that I had the job, the recruiters wanted me to meet with the colleagues who currently worked in the department so everyone would have the opportunity to ask any questions and make sure that I was excited to sign the offer letter. However, scheduling became increasingly difficult. I followed up with the hiring manager multiple times, asking when they would like me to come in, giving additional availability. We scheduled a time, but then it changed again. Then, I got a call that I never thought would happen. They said that the university was going in a different direction, and they were holding off on filling this role. Again, I found myself devastated even more than the first time. This was one of those what's-for-me-will-be-for-me lessons. When people used to tell me that back in the day, I really wanted them to give me some better advice, but this devastating experience was setting me up for a career opportunity that was coming just a few months later. If I had accepted the offer, I wouldn't have even entertained the opportunity that was coming.

That was in September. By December, I had one of the fastest interview processes in my career. Before the holidays, in less than 14 days, I interviewed multiple times, received an offer, and resigned from my current role, and that was how I transitioned into corporate America. That November, my husband had made a contact at a networking event and knew the types of roles that I was researching. He met someone who he knew would be a great contact for me and facilitated an introduction, but we never actually got a chance to speak on the phone. We connected on LinkedIn, exchanged a few emails, and vowed to connect after the holidays. However, a role opened in her company, and she emailed me and said, "I think this is what you're looking for. Would you like to apply? I will send your resume to the hiring manager." They called me the next day, and the process began. Previously, I had been looking for roles in corporate America a little bit here and there, but I wasn't sure if I really wanted to make the transition because so many organizations said that they did not think I would be a great fit since I currently worked in higher education.

Many industries and companies have developed candidate profiles that they gravitate toward because they believe those candidates will have a greater chance of success in the organization. In previous interview processes, I received feedback that the move from higher education to corporate America would be too much of a transition and they needed someone who already "got it." I always clarified my interest and explained how my skills were more than transferable with more "corporate-like" responses, but the hiring managers and recruiters had already made up their minds. However, this particular role was meant for me, and I dodged a major bullet for the director role in higher education that I could never have imagined. Shortly after I moved into corporate America, the career services office at the university that rejected me was significantly restricted in a way that would not have aligned with my career strategy; the team was ultimately downsized and combined with another department.

Sometimes, when you think it's time for you to go, you have to understand that it's the company or organization that is problematic, and it has absolutely nothing to do with your performance.

I could literally write an entire book with every chapter being an interview scenario where I was rejected or declined an offer, and explain what came next. Many times, companies have a whole story behind the role, why it's available, why they can promote or not promote, and you just may not be privy to that information. Of course, you may receive some insider knowledge if you have the right contacts; nevertheless, some circumstances are far beyond your knowledge level. Remain encouraged and committed to moving forward. If it's your time to receive a promotion or an external opportunity, the time will come, maybe not in your time-line, but it will come.

Your Next Move

If you picked up this book, I'm pretty sure you have been looking to take your career to the next level. After all, the book is called *Next Move, Best Move*. So, if you are looking to make your next move, which may mean that you are looking to leave your role or company, I encourage you to go back to the career strategy document in Chapter 13 or go to nextmovebestmovebook.com to download an editable copy and get superclear on the next move you want to make. Be sure that it not only aligns with your skills, experiences, and accomplishments, but that your next role magnifies the work you already accomplished.

How to know when it's time to go isn't just about feeling disgruntled or annoyed, underappreciated, and underpaid. *Knowing when to go is about when you've invested time and energy into your role and an organization, and you know your time has come to an end.* You know that your skills could be used elsewhere to magnify your career strategy and for your own personal and professional development. Keep that in mind as you think about how to apply the best practices in this book. In the next chapter, "Put It All Together," you will receive an outline to take your career strategy forward to ensure your next move is your best move.

Chapter 13

Put It All Together

Career Affirmation: I must believe in myself and my vision; when I do this, I will manifest the career I desire.

You've made it to the end! Now, I invite you to write your strategy directly into this book, go to nextmovebestmove book.com to download an editable copy of the template, or use the next few pages as a guide to copy your strategy into your favorite notebook or planner. Unlike a vision board that may be collecting dust in the corner of your room, I ask that you pull out this document and keep it someplace you will see every week. Check back in with your plan, and continue to refine and edit this document as you grow. *A career strategy is not a document that you put together once and wait for the magic to happen. Think of a career strategy as a fluid body of work that you will continue to reflect on, edit, and revise based on how your career progresses.*

We spend 40-plus hours at work each week, and many of us cannot say that we spend even four hours a week working on our own personal and professional development goals. We end up focusing our energy on our current role, company, or industry situation versus our own experience in the workforce that we are able to control.

You cannot control your boss, co-workers, or even your work-load, but you can control your thoughts, reactions, and actions you take. As I mentioned earlier, back in 2012 I had the unsavory conversation with a former supervisor that literally changed the trajectory of my career. Prior to that time, I believed that my supervisor was supposed to make sure I was considered for salary increases, invite me to participate in new projects, and look out for my overall development. That experience quickly taught me the hard lesson that this was not the case.

Only you can take full responsibility for your own personal and professional development and overall career strategy. It's critical that you invest in experiences that will provide you with the education you need to excel in your career and help you build an unbiased career strategy that supports your long-term vision for your career. This can be books, classes, trainings, workshops, retreats, or conferences.

Building a career in 2021 is very different from building a career in 2010, 2000, 1990, or 1980. There are even new job functions and titles that are less than 10 years old now. When you are thinking about creating your own career strategy, it's easy to skip right to your long-term goals and completely forget about the work that must take place in the middle of where you are now, and where you envision yourself in 5 to 10 years. The middle, in my humble opinion, is where the magic happens. You must outline a combination of step and incremental changes you can make that will move you closer to the long-term vision. And along the way, you'll hit new milestones that should be celebrated; there's no need to wait until you hit the final destination.

As an entrepreneur, you're taught that your product or service must solve the problem of a customer in order for your business to be profitable. Without having a problem to solve, there's no way to market your product or service. However, I find that professionals rarely think of themselves as a product or service to a company. They often market themselves as hardworking team players, but organizations need employees who are able to solve complex problems and increase the company's efficiency.

I also find that professionals generally fall into two categories: specialist or generalist. A specialist has a defined skill that they bring to a work environment while a generalist is a Jack or Jill of all trades. Both have positive and negative attributes, but what's most important is how they relate to your professional brand and the solution that you provide to the company.

Once you get clear on your natural talent, skills, and interests, you can hone in and determine the skills you'd like to magnify in your career development strategy to solve the problem of a company or specific team you're a part of. And remember, the need or gap that you are solving for the company doesn't need to have a catastrophic level of impact; it just needs to be marketable in a way that you and other professionals you interact with understand.

When someone asks what you do, the answer should be simple. Being simple means that it's easy for your mentors, sponsors, peers, and managers to understand so they can help you as you do the work to achieve your professional goals.

One of my favorite exercises to do with clients is a skills assessment. Sure, I know that there are *tons* of assessments you can take to determine what your skills may be based upon your personality, but I like to look at your past experiences to see what skills you currently possess that may be of assistance as you create your own career development plan. When you think about all of your past work experiences, you should be able to compile a list of 5 to 10 skills that you've developed over time. The key here is deciding which skills you would like to maximize in your career and where you may need to do some additional work.

Part of creating your career development strategy is also knowing where you may need to brush up on your skills and invest in personal and professional development. If the skills you'd like to magnify are aligned with the problem you'd like to solve in your industry – you're ready to go! But if the problem you'd like to solve in your industry requires a different skill set, it's time to start investing in your development to ensure that you're able to be competitive in the workforce.

By now I'm sure you're also tired of people telling you the importance of networking. Despite the fact that most professionals know its importance, many still just don't do it. Rather than focus on the number of connections you can build, focus your energy on the number of quality connections you have in your network. One of my mentors uses the term *accelerated collisions* to describe the process of building key relationships through networking. Accelerated collisions are so much more than networking; they are a curated experience where people are able to connect and the process to establish the relationship is expedited so both parties can immediately receive value. My mentor spoke about this term at a retreat that was curated with a room full of professionals and entrepreneurs who were prescreened and primed to build optimal relationships – so it was a room ready for accelerated collisions.

What struck me about this term was that everyone in the room had to make a significant investment to be there. In our careers, many times we invest in doing the work, but not in being in the rooms to magnify the work to external audiences. I've seen professionals attend free or $25 networking events and expect to gain million-dollar connections. Whether you're investing your time or resources, the result will be in proportion to what you invested. Even in your career, you may have to make a larger investment, but you may also receive a much larger reward.

In nearly every speech I give, I end my talk by sharing the importance of becoming relentlessly consistent in order to achieve your goals. *When it comes to career development, no one is going to care more about your career than you.* Working in talent acquisition and helping my clients achieve their professional goals across dozens of industries, I see this more than ever.

Many professionals stay put because they have a great boss who would appear to have no interest in leaving the company…until they surprise you and leave for a better opportunity and you're left trying to figure out your own next steps. Or professionals stay in dead-end jobs because they are afraid of what the "other side" may look like. *What you need to be afraid of is sitting in the same exact place, day after day, month over month, and year over year complaining about the same workplace environment that doesn't align with your goals, while everyone around you is moving and shaking.*

Last but not least, I always recommend leaving a little room for magic to happen. I'm not talking about literal magic, but I believe that when you sow into your career regularly and continuously put in the hard work of mastering your crafts, building relationships, and attacking your gaps, you will be pleasantly surprised by how fast things can move in your career. When you're consistently putting in the work to navigate your career, implement your career strategy, and leave yourself open for unexpected pivots, you will build the career you always wanted. I've seen it happen in my career and in the careers of my clients. Even just 90 days of focus can catapult your career forward if you're intentional with your actions. While studies show it takes the average professional six months to find a new role, exceptions can always be made for excellence. Always leave room for unexpected opportunities that excite you. Additionally, even if you're not currently looking for a new opportunity, your career strategy can assist you in maximizing your current role, as well. This book isn't just about getting a new role; it's about transitioning into a career that you love and that begins with where you are right now.

The career affirmation for this chapter is an edited version of my company's manifesto. I've learned that believing in yourself is step one and the most important step you must make if you would like to achieve any goal in your life. We discussed your career in this book, so I refocused the affirmation to reflect that.

Again, if you picked up this book and read it up until this point, I know you care about your career trajectory. Now, it's time to move from caring about your career to believing that the career you desire is possible and then going after it!

Your next, best move is to take what you've learned and apply it in your career. Transitioning to a career you love is truly about creating a strategy to take you from where you are to exactly where you would like to be. On the next few pages, you'll see a template that can be used to create your career strategy or you can go to nextmovebestmovebook.com to download an editable copy of the template with a one-page overview that will allow you to add also fill in your key strengths, growth opportunities, ideal work environment, core values, and 10-year vision.

Your Next Move

Core Values:			
Current State *Where you would like your career to be at this time in the future?* *You can list an actual role/ title or your updated talent designation that was shared in Chapter 4.*	**Current State**	**6 months**	**1 year**
Gap *Your personal and/or professional area of focus to move your career to the next level.*	**Gap**	**Gap**	**Gap**
Milestone/Achievement *This milestone lets you know you are ready to move onto the next phase of your career strategy. If you are ready to move on in more or less than six months increments, that's fine, too!*	**Milestone/ Achievement**	**Milestone/ Achievement**	**Milestone/ Achievement**
Tasks *These are the individual tasks that you will work on in this 6- to 12-month stretch.*	**Tasks**	**Tasks**	**Tasks**

Last Edited:			
18 months	2 years	3 years	5 years
Gap	Gap	Gap	Gap
Milestone/ Achievement:	Milestone/ Achievement	Milestone/ Achievement	Milestone/ Achievement
Tasks	Tasks	Tasks	Tasks

Putting together this career strategy is step one in making your next move your best move, but it will not happen by osmosis. You must diligently apply the best practices shared throughout each page of this book and do the work to become a leader in your industry.

I also highly recommend doing your own roadshow after your career strategy is completed. When senior-level executives move into a new role, they frequently do a roadshow or "listening tour" to meet with all of the key stakeholders who drive the day-to-day work in their new organization or team. The purpose of this time is to deeply understand how their role impacts the organization, the changes that need to be made, and to build relationships with the stakeholders who will be pivotal in moving the work forward. After this time, the executive is armed with the information to create or update the strategy for their organization. Your experience reading this book and completing the "Your Next Move" exercises should be similar. You've completed several exercises and likely reached out to professionals in your field to gain the information needed to create your career strategy. Now that the strategy is completed, it's important to go back out to your manager, mentors, peers, and sponsors to talk about where you'd like to go in your career.

Professionals in your network will not be able to advocate for you if they have no idea where you'd like to go. Over the past few years, I've conducted dozens of workshops on advocating for yourself in the workplace and found that many people think that's just about speaking up for yourself. *Sure, you can advocate for yourself when you disagree with something, but you can also advocate for yourself when you want to position yourself as a leader in the workplace.* Positioning yourself in the workplace truly comes from having a strategic plan and exhibiting the leadership behaviors that back up your career strategy.

Several times in this book, I've shared the following three pieces of advice from my father.

1. Work hard and focus on being the best at whatever you do.
2. Excellence is always important; be excellent.
3. If they hit you first, hit back.

We never got a chance to talk about point number 3. *When something happens in your career and you "take a hit," your strategy is the way you hit them back. For every time you've been underestimated, allow your hard work, constant pursuit of excellence in your career, and increasing growth to hit them back.*

Early on in my career, I used to wait tables at a chain restaurant because my full-time salary didn't pay all of my bills. I never felt shame from working as a server. In fact, I enjoyed the camaraderie and the wad of cash that I walked out with every night after my shift. On the day I finally resigned from that job, after transitioning into a full-time job that aligned with my career goals and paid a salary that I could fully live on, I'll never forget that the restaurant manager looked me in the eyes, chuckled, and said, "You'll be back. Y'all always come back."

They underestimated me. I'm struggling not to call their name out in this story because (a) it's petty and (b) for every person who's ever underestimated my abilities to take my career and life to the next level, their low predictions of my abilities never came to fruition. Although I know I have always had a drive toward excellence, there is also a piece of me that chuckles and says, "Look at me now." My continued success and impact is the ultimate "hit back."

My hope is that the advancement of your career will be a continuous process you embark on so that you are always ready for the next move, or better yet, the next move finds you.

Acknowledgments

Writing a book is something I always wanted to do, but I didn't think I would have the opportunity to do it. The mere fact that you, yes you, are currently holding this book in your hands that I put together is crazy to me. While this book is dedicated to the professionals who need this information, this book is also dedicated to my husband Kevin, Mom, Dad, sister Michelle, and Godmother, who challenge me to "keep pushing" – and always hit back. I would also like to acknowledge my hometown neighbor and second mother, Noreen, who celebrates my accomplishments like I'm one of her children, as well as my biological mom, Shanalyn, whom I know is holding onto this book with pride and sharing it in her salon.

I would also like to dedicate this book to the professionals who have inspired and challenged me throughout my career. Every professional experience I've had has inspired me to either change how I would approach a similar situation in the future or adapt a positive behavior into my professional development.

I would like to highlight a few of the mentors and professionals who have invested their time into helping me get this exact moment: Amber Lennon, for being my first "work bestie" – I miss our office dance parties; Lejorne Leys, for being my favorite personal and professional sounding board – always reminding me to not to be petty; Taryn Duffy, for teaching me what it looks like to support your team unapologetically, even if it means you have to take heat from leadership; Hayley Hedgpeth, for being the absolute best teammate and confirming my love of being a people leader; Jason Cascone, for challenging me to strive for more in my first career development role; Kathleen O'Keefe, for introducing me to the power of professional associations; and Jasmine B. Hawthorne, for always leading by example and knowing exactly how to handle high-pressure conversations in the workplace.

It's also important for me to note the mentors I've acquired throughout the years who have donated their time and attention to help me navigate the world of work in the same manner I hope this book will help you: Lindsey Pollak, Andrew Ceperley, W. Rochelle Calhoun, Dawn Carter, William Clyde, Susan Chapman-Hughes, and Dr. Sherri Cole-Perkins, and so many more I know I'm forgetting to mention.

I'd also like to thank Laci Swann of Sharp Editorial for helping me edit and fine-tune this book to perfection. You're not just a book editor, you are the partner in crime to this book and to me as an author. I look forward to working with you as *Next Move, Best Move* becomes a full career development series. (Yes, I'm manifesting that now!)

Last but not least, I also have to mention my eight-year-old nephew, Kevyn, who said I could not write a whole book without writing "a few pages" about him. While you haven't landed your first job yet, Kevyn, I truly hope that this book will help you when it's your time in 2028 when you're in high school or 2032 when you graduate from college.

To anyone who has ever connected with me in the workplace or through my company, Manifest Yourself, thank you.

Index

Abilities, feelings vs., 148–149
Abundance, leaving room for, 69
Accelerated collisions, 189–190
Accepting job offers, 166–167
Accomplishments:
    identifying core values from,
        52–54
    interview conversations based on, 166
    on win list, 170–171
Accountability, for personal development,
    79–80
Achievements, on career strategy
    document, 192, 193
Actions, professional brand and,
    121–122
Admissions counselor position, 37–39
Advocacy. *See also* Self-advocacy
    branding and, 125, 194
    by sponsors, 97
Alignment:
    of branding and goals, 123–124, 126
    maintaining, with long-term
        vision, 62

of mission statement, brand, and
    vision, 140–141
of opportunity with core values, 50–52
Alumni networks, 98–99
Angelou, Maya, 81
Annual reviews, 4–6
Anxiety, about speaking up, 148–151
Assessment. *See also* Self-assessment
    career, 160
    of opportunity's alignment with core
        values, 50–52
    skills, 189
Assistant director of admissions position,
    50, 162
At-will employment, 138
Authenticity, 91
Authority, elevating, 114. *See also*
    Speaking up

Baby boomers, 77
Behaviors:
    of great managers, 16–17
    managing up to change, 20–22

Believing in yourself, 191
Benefits:
    reviewing, with job offers, 166, 168
    in salary negotiations, 164–165
Beyoncé, 134
Bias, in performance feedback, 110–112
Black Student Union, 30
Black women:
    biased performance feedback
        for, 111–112
    fears about speaking up for, 149
    in leadership positions, 59
Boredom, 177
Brand:
    alignment of mission statement, vision,
        and, 140–141
    in career strategy, 114
    consistency in, 120, 140–141
    as factor in hiring, 123–124, 160
    how you show up as, 124
    internal and external elements
        of, 121–123
    outside of current job, 137–138
    promoting, 5–6
    and salary negotiation, 157
    sharing work and, 133–137
Branding, see Personal and profes-
    sional branding
Brand manifesto, 124, 139–140
Bridge roles, 82
Bridging gaps, 75–84
    to achieve long-term vision, 81–83
    career affirmation, 74
    career development plan for, 189
    and hard work/excellence
        mindset, 75–76
    personal growth and development
        for, 78–80
    self-assessment of strengths and
        weaknesses for, 113
    for strategic career transitions, 76–78
Brown, Brené, 153
Budget, target salary range and, 163, 164
Business coaches, 127–128

Camaraderie, 45–47, 195
"Cancel" culture, 148
Candidate profiles, 182
Career:
    continuous process of advanc-
        ing in, 195
    getting first-hand accounts
        of, 60, 69–70
    longevity of, 34–35, 61
    progression of, 34–35
    seasons in, 8–9, 22–23, 92, 105
    selecting a, 60
    taking control of your, 176–177
    working a job vs. building a, 2–4
Career assessment, 160
Career Counselor Technology Forum, 88
Career decision-making:
    about leaving your job, 175–177
    intentionality and happiness in, 38–39
    self-assessment in, 32–35
Career development counselor position,
    2–6, 60–62, 133–134
Career development plan, 187–195
    applying lessons to, 191, 194
    building key relationships in, 189–190
    career affirmation, 186
    career strategy document in,
        187–188, 192–194
    from employer, 67, 109–110, 112
    for high performers, 20
    for high-potential talent, 110–112
    and "hitting back" with
        excellence, 195
    leaving room for unexpected
        opportunities in, 190–191
    problem-solving mindset for, 188–189
    roadshow in, 194
    self-advocacy in, 194
    skills assessment for, 189
    taking responsibility for development
        with, 187
    using, to grow in current role, 190
Career profile presentation, 170
Career-related conversations, 40–41, 106

Career strategy, 105–115
  and bias in performance feedback,
    110–112
  building relationships to support,
    94–99
  career affirmation, 104
  "get in and figure it out" as, 51
  incorporating feedback on, 9
  incorporating others' tactics in, 9
  insider information for building,
    105–106, 108–110
  key elements of, 113–114
  before leaving a job, 177
  and long-term vision, 68
  for managers, 23
  taking responsibility for, 2,
    108–110, 187
  of undergraduates/recent gradu-
    ates, 30–32
  understanding work and organization
    to build, 106–108
Career strategy document:
  assessing gaps with, 125–127
  clarifying next more with, 183
  core values on, 54–55
  creating, 114
  goals on, 68–70
  revisiting, 114–115, 187–188,
    192–194
  template for, 55, 69, 113, 187,
    191–194
Career trajectory:
  asking direct reports about, 19
  changing, 1
  conversation with manager/skip leader
    about, 175
  identifying gaps from others', 82
  taking responsibility for your, 22–23
Career transition(s). See also Strategic
    career transition(s)
  checking alignment of brand with, 123
  defined, xi
  fear about, 190
  lateral (see Lateral career transitions)

non-strategic, 64–65
promotional (see Promotional career
    transitions)
reflecting before next, 7–9
"right" or "wrong," 9
time-in-role as basis for, 64, 75, 76
unforeseen, 138
Chain of command, 82
Challenges, appropriate level of,
    113–114
Character, 121
Close relationships, 49, 93
Coaches:
  building relationships with, 95–96
  business, 127–128
  insider information from, 108–110
Code-switching, 120, 140–141
Cold calls, 48
Collisions, accelerated, 189–190
Common interest, bonding over, 91
Communication:
  about transferable skills, 35–37, 40–41
  career-related conversations,
    40–41, 106
  difficult conversations, 147–148, 170
  follow-up, 152–153
  to maintain relationships, 94
  of mission statement, 140
  in relationship building, 91
  of salary range, 162–163
  speaking up for deeper, 147–148
Comparable job titles and salary
    ranges, 161–165
Conferences:
  building relationships at, 136
  sharing brand at, 136–137
  sharing work at, 133–135
Conflict, leaving a job due to, 178–179
Connecticut, 3, 159
Connections with professionals:
  quality of, 189–190
  to share work, 135–137
Conny Spalding (character), 29–30, 33,
    59, 60, 159

Consistency, 120, 140–141, 190
Contacts, opening networks of, 90–92
Control, 176–177, 187
Core values, 45–55
    career affirmation, 44
    on career strategy document, 192, 193
    character and, 121
    evaluating opportunity's alignment
        with, 50–52
    from greatest accomplishments and
        do-better moments, 52–54
    identifying, in poorly-fitting
        environment, 45–50
    and mission statement, 139–140
    self-advocacy to stay true to,
        151–152
Courage, 153
COVID-19 pandemic, 93, 108, 133,
    138, 161, 179
Credibility, 139
Curiosity mindset, 4

Deadlines, meeting, 145–149
Decision-making, *see* Career
    decision-making
Destiny's Child, 134
Difficult conversations, 147–148, 170
Director of career services position,
    60–62, 70
Disagreements, self-advocacy in, 151, 194
Do-better moments:
    defined, 52
    finding commonalities in, 153–154
    identifying core values from, 52–54
    involving speaking up, 152–154

Education, as core value, 50
Educational experience, 70–71, 81
Effort, 68–69, 194
Email, 145–147, 171
Employer:
    career development plan from, 67,
        109–110, 112
    expanding brand outside of, 137–138

Entrepreneurs and entrepreneurship,
    111–112, 127–128, 188
Entry-level employment, 32–33
Excellence, 194
    and bridging gaps, 75–76
    as core value, 139, 140
    "hitting back" with, 195
    and relationship building, 87, 93
Executive assistant, 95
Expectation-setting, for salary
    negotiation, 157–158
Experience. *See also* Past experiences
    as basis for brand, 121–123
    bridging gaps with, 81–82
    leveraging another's, 127–128
    managerial, 70–71, 137
    skills vs., 122
    speaking to your unique, 149–150
    of yourself, in branding, 119–120,
        124, 125
External elements, of brand, 121–123
Extracurricular activities, 30–31, 34

Failures, *see* Do-better moments
Fast Company, 139
Fear, 170, 190
Feedback:
    bias in, 110–112
    on career strategy, 9
    from coaches, 96
    to identify brand, 125–126
    to identify gaps, 75–76, 80
    positive, 171
Feelings, abilities vs., 148–149
Financial advice, from clients, 46–47
First-hand accounts, of career, 60, 69–70
First-hand experience, mentors with, 96
Follow-up communication, 152–153
Formal mentorship agreements, 96
Fulfillment, 50

Gaps in experience or skills. *See also*
    Bridging gaps
    and brand, 124–127

on career strategy document,
125–127, 192, 193
Gatekeepers, 95
Gender pay gap, 157–158
Generalists, 18, 188
Generation X, 77
Geographic area:
with limited career opportunities,
161–162
setting target salary based on, 161
"Get in and figure it out" strategy, 51
Glass ceiling, 180
Glassdoor, 162
Goals. *See also* Short-term goals
alignment of branding and,
123–124, 126
on career strategy document,
68–70
effort and size of, 68–69
making career transitions
without, 61–62
Goal setting, 59–71
career affirmation, 58
creating long-term vision, 66–69
figuring out where you are now
for, 62–66
information interviews for
short-term, 69–71
information needed for
long-term, 59–61
Goldsmith, Marshall, 92
Google, 162
Graduate students:
benefits of internships for, 45
career transitions for, xi
Growth:
to bridge gaps, 78–80
in current role, 190
leaving jobs that do not support,
175
outgrowing your work, 178

Happiness:
core value alignment and, 50

leaving a job to pursue, 176, 179
seeking, 38–39
Hard work, 194
and bridging gaps, 75–76
and relationship building, 87,
93, 107–108
and sharing work, 134
"Hell-no" number, 163–164
High-achieving professionals (high
performers), 20, 80, 169
High-potential talent, 110–112
Hiring:
brand as factor in, 123–124, 160
salary negotiation during, 124–125
self-advocacy during, 166–167
of specialists, 18
toolkit as basis for, 160
"Hitting back," 75, 87, 194, 195
Holistic relationships, 92, 99
Hopelessness, 76–77
Human resources team, 108, 169, 179

Impact:
career transitions based on, 64–65
of marketable skills, 188–189
and salary negotiation, 65–66
sharing work to increase, 135
of speaking up for your team, 148
Industry(-ies):
conditions in, when leaving a job,
175
switching, 37–39, 164
Inequities, workplace, 76–77,
157–158
Influence, 2
Informational interviews:
asking for connections in, 90–91
assessing core value alignment in, 51
identifying experience gaps in,
81–82
identifying skills gaps in, 77–78
for short-term goal setting, 69–71
vetting new opportunities with,
109

Insider information:
  for building career strategy,
    105–106, 108–110
  defined, 106
  on new opportunities, 108–110
  on organizational constraints, 182–183
  in relationships, 93
Intentionality, 37, 38, 51
Internal elements, of brand, 121–123
Internships, 29–32, 45
Interpersonal conflict, 178–179
Interviews, *see* Informational interviews;
  Job interviews
Investment:
  in networking, 190
  in personal development, 79–80

Jobs:
  building a career vs. working at, 2–4
  recycling, 51, 76
Job application process, 6, 9, 35–36.
  See also Hiring
Job candidate profiles, 182
Job interviews:
  communicating transferable
    skills in, 41
  discussing strengths and weaknesses
    in, 119–120
  mentality for, 123–124
  questions about leadership in, 24
  receiving a job offer while participat-
    ing in, 166–167
  strategies for, 166
Job offers, 165–168, 180–183
Job titles, 161–165, 169, 188

Keeping in touch, 92–94
Keywords, associating yourself with, 41
Kimberlybcummings.com, 40, 55, 69,
  113, 183, 187, 191

Lateral career transitions, xi
  after outgrowing work, 178

bridging skills gaps for, 76, 78
employer career development
  planning for, 67
learning new skills in, 64
Leader(s). *See also* Managers
  managing up to influence, 20–22
  positioning yourself as, 2, 194
  rapport building by, 19–20
  relationships with, 88–92
  skip, 147–148, 175
  speaking up to, 147–148
  value of relationship building for, 88
Leadership, 15–24
  career affirmation, 14
  development of team in, 17–20
  managing up, 20–22
  as privilege, 14–17
  professional and personal development
    for, 78–79
  in professional organizations, 135–136
  and responsibility for your career
    trajectory, 22–23
  in your role, 2
Learning, from do-better
  moments, 153–154
Leaving your job, 175–183
  career affirmation, 174
  career trajectory conversation
    before, 175
  and clarifying next more with career
    strategy document, 183
  common reasons for, 22–23,
    39, 177–180
  due to workplace inequity, 77
  securing a new opportunity
    before, 180–183
  as strategic career decision, 176–177
Lee, Barbara Ross, 180
Letters of recommendation, 92–93
Life stage, career support for, 179–180
LinkedIn:
  articulating your value on, 160
  assessing skill set with, 39

building relationships with, 89, 99, 182
mission and profile summary
on, 124, 140
research for goal setting on, 69–70
research for salary negotiation
on, 161, 162
Listening tours, 194
Lobby, working the, 47–48
Longevity, career, 34–35, 61
Long Island, N.Y., 30, 31, 36, 45–50
Long-term vision:
alignment of mission, brand,
and, 140–141
bridging gaps to achieve, 81–83
in career strategy, 114
changes in, 69
creating, 66–69
and figuring out where you are, 62–66
information needed for, 59–61
making transitions without, 61–62
Loss, from not negotiating salary, 158

"Making moves in silence" mindset, 134
Management:
leadership and, 2
managing up, 20–22
as privilege, 14–17
Managers. *See also* Leader(s)
behaviors of great, 16–17
biased feedback from, 110–112
career strategy from, 108
career trajectory conversation
with, 175
difficult conversations with, 147–148
roadshow with, 194
salary negotiation with, 169–170
sharing sentiments with, 145–147
Managerial experience, 70–71, 137
Manifest Yourself, 111–112, 139–140, 191
Marketable skills, 188–189
Marketing analyst position, 32–34,
87, 159–160
MBTI (Myers–Briggs Type Indicator), 33

Mental transition, as career transition, xi
Mentors:
building relationships with, 90–92, 96
career strategies from, 108
insider information from, 108–110
offline branding with, 125
roadshow with, 194
Metropolitan New York College Career
Planning Officers Association
(MNYCCPOA), 88
Milestones, 62, 192, 193
"Millennial" mindset, leaving a job
in, 77, 175
Missed opportunities, 83–84
Mission, 133–141
and brand outside of current
job, 137–138
career affirmation, 132
connecting with professionals to
share, 135–137
and core values, 139–140
sharing work and brand, 133–135
Mission statement, 138–141
Mistakes, repeating, 6
MNYCCPOA (Metropolitan New York
College Career Planning Officers
Association), 88
Motivation, 59–61
Moving expenses, 168
Mulan (film), 149
Myers–Briggs Type Indicator (MBTI), 33

National Association of Colleges and
Employers (NACE) Leadership
Advancement Program, 90, 92
Negotiating salary, *see* Salary negotiation
Networking:
accelerated collisions from, 189–190
to build relationships, 87–92
with leaders/power players, 88–92
opening of contacts' networks, 90–92
and post-graduate employment, 31–34
repeating mistakes in, 6

New Role, New Experience
designation, 64, 65
New Role, New Skills designation, 63
New York, N.Y., 3, 31, 33, 88,
151, 161, 163
New York State Cooperative and
Experiential Education Association
(NYSCEEA), 77–78, 88, 134–138

Offline branding, 125
Online branding, 124–125
The Oprah Winfrey Show
(television series), 139
Outgrowing work, 178

Past experiences, 29–42
assessing skill set acquired in, 39–41
career affirmation, 28
in internships, 29–32
knowledge from outside, 81
of professionals in your goal
position, 70–71
and self-assessment in career
decision-making, 32–35
shaping of career by, 92
transferable skills from,
35–37, 159–160
when switching industries, 37–39
PayScale, 162
Peers:
building relationships with, 95
insider information from, 108–110
roadshow with, 194
People leaders, *see* Leaders
People of color. *See also* Black women
career development plans for, 110
code-switching and brand consistency
for, 140–141
leadership development for, 139–140
"making moves in silence"
mindset for, 134
recognition for, 176
Performance-based salary
increases, 3–6, 176

Performance feedback:
bias in, 110–112
in career trajectory conversation, 175
identifying brand based on, 125–126
Performance standards, 5
Personal and professional branding,
119–128
assessing gaps with career strategy
document, 125–127
building relationships and, 89
career affirmation, 118
code-switching and, 120
for generalists, 18
goal-setting and, 61, 123–124
and how you show up at work, 124
internal and external elements of
brand, 121–123
leveraging another's experience
with, 127–128
opening closed doors with, 123–124
outside of current job, 137–138
relationship building for self-
promotion vs., 119–120
in salary negotiation, 124–125
sharing your brand, 133–134
Personal banker position,
34–37, 45–48, 87
Personal circumstances, changes in,
leaving job due to, 180
Personal development, 6
identifying areas for, 189
investment in, 67, 79–80, 187
for leadership, 78–79
leaving jobs that do not support, 175
taking responsibility for, 187
"Playing small," 41, 68–69, 83,
149–150
Poorly-fitting environment, identifying
core values in, 45–50
Power players, 88–92
Presentations, 133–135, 170
Presentation skills, 159
Problem-solving mindset, 188–189
Productivity, satisfaction and, 19

Professional branding, *see* Personal and professional branding
Professional development, 6
  bridging gaps with, 78–79
  identifying areas for, 189
  investment in, 67, 187
  as leader's responsibility, 15–20
  managing up to ensure, 20–21
  to prepare for leadership, 78–79
  pursuit of, in professional brand, 122
  taking responsibility for your own, 187
  of team, 17–20
Professional organizations:
  informational interviews with members of, 77–78
  managerial experience in, 137
  networking in, 88–89
  for professionals in your goal position, 70–71
  promoting your work in, 135–137
  value of membership in, 90
Professional value, *see* Value
Promotional career transitions, xi
  after outgrowing work, 178
  employer's career development planning for, 67, 109–110
  identifying gaps preventing, 76, 78, 126, 127
  salary negotiation for, 168–169
Publishing industry internship, 31–32
Punctuality, 121–122

Quitting, *see* Leaving your job

Rapport building, by leaders, 19–20
Real estate comps, 161
Recent graduates:
  alumni network, 98–99
  career longevity for, 34
  career strategy for, 30–32
  skill set assessment for, 39
Recognition, waiting for, 176
Recommendations, giving, 92–93

Recruiters and recruiting, 105, 124–125, 127
Reflection:
  before career transition, 7–9
  on core values, 51–52
  to determine next steps, 33
  on do-better moments, 152–154
  on manager relationships, 23–24
  before salary negotiation, 170–171
Rejecting salary offers, 163–164
Relationships, 87–99
  career affirmation, 86
  close, 49, 93
  effect of speaking up on, 148
  focusing on quality of, 189–190
  holistic, 92, 99
  keeping in touch to maintain, 92–94
  with leaders/power players, 88–92
  and leaving your job, 175
  with managers, 23–24
  with mentors, coaches, and sponsors, 22
  opening of contact's networks in, 90–92
  to support career strategy, 94–99
  in unforeseen career transitions, 138
  in virtual environments, 93–94
Relationship building:
  to bridge gaps, 83
  in career development plan, 189–190
  in career strategy, 106–108
  at conferences, 136
  as core value, 49–50
  networking for, 87–92
  roadshows for, 194
  for self-promotion vs. branding, 119–120
  with thought leaders, 80
Remote learning, 133
Resigning, *see* Leaving your job
Resilience, 139

Responsibility:
    for career strategy, 2, 108–110, 187
    for career trajectory, 22–23
    for professional development of
        others, 15–20
    for your own personal/professional
        development, 187
Retaliation, fear of, 147, 148
Rhimes, Shonda, 89
Right Role, New Skills designation,
    63, 75
Right Role, Right Time designation,
    63, 75
Rite of passage, management
    opportunity as, 15
Roadmap, for team, 17, 65–66
Roadshow, 194
Rohn, Jim, 175
Role mastery, boredom after, 177
Role models, 97

Salary:
    early career decisions based on, 30–33
    leaving job due to, 178
    performance-based increases
        in, 3–6, 176
    reduction in, when switching
        industries, 38–39
Salary negotiation, 157–171
    assessing your value for, 158–160
    career affirmation, 156
    impact and results as basis for, 65–66
    personal and professional brand
        in, 124–125
    preparing for, 168–170
    reflecting on "wins" prior to, 170–171
    self-advocacy in, 151
    setting expectation for, 157–158
    value of role and benefits in, 161–165
Salary negotiation conversation:
    disclosing budget in, 163
    preparing for, 169–170
    setting expectations prior to, 157
    strategy for, 166–168

Salary ranges, researching, 161–165
Sales goals, 36–37, 46–49
San Francisco, Calif., 161
Satisfaction, work, 19, 50
Scandal (television series), 89
Scarcity mindset, 150
Seasons in career, 8–9, 22–23, 92, 105
Second-degree contacts, 51
Self-advocacy:
    in career development plan, 194
    failure in, 4, 6
    in hiring process, 166–167
    in salary negotiations, 151
    and speaking up, 150–152
Self-assessment:
    in career decision-making, 32–35
    for personal development, 79
    of professional value, 159–160
    of skill set acquired in past
        experience, 39–41
    of strengths and weaknesses,
        113–114, 119–120
    of transferable skills, 37–38
Self-promotion, 89, 119–120, 135–137
Senior-level executives, roadshows
    for, 194
Sentiments, sharing, 145–148
Shanté Smith (character), 29–30, 33,
    59, 60, 159
Short-term goals:
    bridging gaps to achieve, 81–82
    on career strategy document, 114, 188
    information interviews for setting,
        69–71
    and long-term vision, 68
    as milestones, 62, 192, 193
    motivation from, 59–61
Showing up, branding and, 124
Side hustles, 111–112, 122
Sign-on bonus, 168
Sister Circle Live (television series), 150
Skill-based interview conversations, 166
Skills assessment, for career
    development plan, 189

Skill set:
  assessing acquired, 39–41
  coaches for building, 95–96
  gaps in (*see* Gaps in experience
    or skills)
  marketable skills in, 188–189
  and personal/professional
    branding, 120
  for positions with ambiguous
    requirements, 31–32
  and professional brand, 121–123
  of professionals in your goal position,
    70–71
  salary comparison based on, 162–163
Skip leaders, 147–148, 175
Small, playing, 41, 68–69, 83, 149–150
Speaking up, 145–154
  anxiety about, 148–150
  career affirmation, 144
  and conversations about sentiments vs.
    execution, 145–148
  in follow-up communication, 152–153
  reflecting on do-better moments
    involving, 152–154
  self-advocacy for, 150–152
  for your team, 148, 152
Specialists, 18, 188
Sponsors, 97, 108–110, 194
Standing up for yourself, *see* Speaking up
Strategic career transition(s):
  alignment with core values in, 50–52
  bridging gaps for, 76–78
  communicating about skills in, 41
  creating potential
    opportunities with, 42
  impact and, 64–65
  leaving your job as, 175–177
  preparing for, 83–84, 127–128
  switching industries as, 37–39
  transitions without goals vs., 61–62
  uncertainty about, 1
Strengths, self-assessment of,
    113–114, 119–120
StrengthsFinder assessment, 33

Stretch assignments, 64, 113–114, 148–150
Student Affairs award ceremony,
    32–33, 158–159
Successor, following in shoes of, 65–66

Target salary range, 161–165, 167–168
Tasks, on career strategy document,
    192, 193
Task execution:
  conversations about, 145–148
  as "doing your job," 15
  generalists as drivers of, 18
  impact in, 65–66
  performance feedback on, 112
Team:
  responsibility for professional
    development of, 17–20
  speaking up for your, 148, 152
Teamwork, as core value, 48
Testimonials, 171
"Time-in-role" basis for transition,
    64, 75, 76
Toolkit, defined, 160
Transferable skills:
  assessing your, 39–41
  communicating, 35–37, 40–41
  and professional value, 159–160
  when switching industries, 37–39
Tuition assistance, 165
Two Can Play That Game (film),
    29–30, 59, 60

Underestimated, being, 195
Undergraduates:
  alumni networks for, 98
  benefits of internships for, 45
  career strategy for, 30–32
  career transitions for, xi
Unexpected opportunities, leaving room
    for, 190–191

Value:
  articulating your, 35–36, 138–139,
    158–160, 170

Value (*Continued*)
assessing, for salary negotiation, 158–160
of your role, 161–165, 168
Values, core, *see* Core values
Virtual environments, maintaining
relationships in, 93–94, 108
Vision, *see* Long-term vision
Vision boards, 66–67, 187
Voice, using, *see* Speaking up
Vulnerability, 153

Warm introductions, 87, 89–91
Washington, Kerry, 89
Waterford, Conn., 34
Weaknesses, self-assessment of,
113–114, 119–120

Webinar fatigue, 93
Westchester County, N.Y., 136
Winfrey, Oprah, 97, 139
Win list, 170–171
"Wins," reflecting on, 170–171
Women. *See also* Black women
career development plans for, 110
code-switching and brand consistency
for, 140–141
leadership development for, 139–140
recognition for, 176
salary negotiation for, 157–158
Work, understanding the role of
your, 106–108
Working the lobby, 47–48
Work satisfaction, 19, 50